THE BOOKS OF
GEORGE JEAN NATHAN

∽ ∽

PASSING JUDGMENTS

PASSING

Judgments

•

by GEORGE JEAN NATHAN

ALFRED · A · KNOPF

NEW YORK · 1935

FOR

SEAN O'CASEY

Contents

ৎ ৎ

PASSING JUDGMENTS

As One Critic to Another

∽ ∽

1

It is the mark of the very young critic to regard praise as a symptom of weakness.

2

The tolerance that often comes to a critic in his later years is simply the result of a belated consciousness of the complete and utter unimportance of nine-tenths of the persons and performances he is brought to criticize. Its synonym is indifference.

3

The quality of a critic is best to be appraised by the quality of his enemies. To analyze his worth it is only necessary to analyze the worth of those who detest him.

4

To demand a consistent and invariable dignity of criticism is ridiculous. There is a place for dignity and a place for low roughhouse. What is more absurd than a dignified and austere approach to rubbish?

5

The cocksure critic may sometimes be an ass, but at least he is always more readable than the perhaps sounder critic given to hesitations, doubts, and qualifications. It may be too bad, but it is, alas, true.

6

A smooth, vigorous and stimulating style may contrive to give a second-rate critic the convincing aspect of a first-rater.

7

Critics are fond of defending themselves against the allegation that their verdicts are sometimes colored by their immediate mood, state of health, etc. They assert that their judgments are not affected by such things and that their minds remain clear, calm and equitable even when their wives or best girls have just been run over by street-cars, their children been bitten by cinnamon bears at the zoo, their banks have closed, and they themselves are the victims of dreadful bellyaches. But they lie, and they know it. There doubtless never lived a critic whose opinions were not at one time or another influenced by the way he felt at the moment he was passing judgment.

8

It is a favorite professorial belief that the more broadly informed and educated the critic, the better a critic he will be. This is largely bosh. It avails the critic of literature, drama, painting, or music nothing at all to be a ranking scholar in astronomy, geology, calculus, Egyptology, or any one or all of a score of such extrinsic subjects. If he knows thoroughly his own trade, that is enough — and he will be a good enough critic to suit anyone. There is no more reason to demand that he be richly equipped in a lot of other directions than there is to demand that a good pianist be a Bachelor of Science, or a master plumber a Phi Beta Kappa.

9

We frequently hear it said that a critic should never indulge in personalities; that such indulgence is beneath the high art of criticism and woefully cheapens it. Here, also, we engage a pretty nosegay of nonsense. The practitioner of an art is often as properly the subject of criticism and comment as the art he practises. To keep personalities out of criticism of musical performances or dramatic performances, for example, is to insist that the critic not leave his study and confine his remarks to the music script or the printed play. Criticism of painting may be rid of personalities and so, to a lesser extent, may criticism of certain forms of literature. But, in general, criticism that sedulously avoids personalities is like a novel whose characters are sketched merely in the flat.

10

The word *katharsis* has been responsible for more lovely buncombe in criticism than any five hundred or thousand other words all rolled together.

11

A fine style consists in a fine mind filtered through the graces of the written word. Too much of what easily passes today for fine style consists merely in the graces of the written word filtered through utter hollowness and vacuity.

12

Overly radical opinion in critical writing is sometimes simply a cloak wherewith the critic seeks to conceal from his readers, and often from himself, his temporary incompetence in perhaps sounder and more orthodox channels, his inability to make calm rationality interesting, and his passing mental staleness.

13

It is the first duty and mark of the successful critic to be as sure of himself in public as he is now and then unsure of himself in private.

14

Why is it that among the great artists of the world, whether male or female, we find so few blondes?

15

The pointing out by a critic of errors in the writings of a fellow-critic is held to be against the punctilio and all union rules, and is regarded as being somewhat offensive. There seems to be an unwritten law among critics that they should stand more or less together and that if one of them, either in or out of his cups, commits some such boner, say, as attributing " Œdipus at Colonos " to Mr. Samuel Shipman or the Hattons, it is the friendly duty of all the rest of the boys to keep politely mum about it. To call attention to the bull is apparently bad sportsmanship, and the act of a cad.

16

The lack of respect which a considerable number of people have for the dramatic critic is due in no small part to the critic himself. If lawyers, doctors and other professional men conducted themselves as the average dramatic critic is in the habit of doing, people would not have much respect for them either. No one would think for a moment of approaching a lawyer or a doctor, with whom he had but the slightest acquaintance, and asking him for free advice as to legal or medical matters. What is more, if anyone were so presumptuous, the lawyer or doctor would quickly put him in his place — or subsequently send him a good round bill for the imparted counsel. The dramatic critic, however, has no such professional pride. Anyone, apparently, is privileged to come up to him at any time and ask him anything about matters to which he has devoted a lifetime of professional study, meditation and experience. Without charging a cent, he will answer questions as to what he thinks of this actor or that; as to what plays he recommends, and why; as to the theatre in England, France, Germany, Italy, Russia and the Congo Free State; as to his ideas about playwriting; as to anything, in short, that any forward and impudent person may wish to know. And as no person has much respect for anything that he can get for nothing, the dramatic critic comes to be respected just about as much as a street peddler of hand-bills.

17

People have a way of attributing to the critic the triviality that often inheres in his working materials. He may have no straw, yet it is expected of him that he fashion bricks. For certain readers somehow always imagine that the art of the drama persists mysteriously and immediately, even *in vacuo,* and that it is the duty of the serious and sober critic to discern and expatiate upon it, in concrete detail, though it may be nowhere in evidence. The critic who, having no authentic drama to deal with, deals with what he finds in terms of transitory journalism, is declared lacking in weight and in lofty ideals.

18

It is, and ever has been, the common fallacy of immediate criticism to credit the pioneer and innovator in any

[8]

form of art with high æsthetic virtues which subsequent calm, reflective criticism often finds he has been without.

19

The commonest interrogation of a dramatic critic in long practice is as to how he can possibly go on writing about the theatre for so many years, the implication being that one can say all there is to say about the theatre and drama in something like two or three months. The question, I find, is usually posed by men who have devoted their entire lives to writing about next wars in the Pacific, or local politics, or the dreadful state of culture in Arkansas, or some other such topic. The theatre, it seems to me, is as various as the world its drama reflects, and as constantly changing. Not the cheap, popular, box-office theatre, to be sure, but the theatre of the better sort. And that theatre has in late years shown a steady growth and a steady development.

Every writer must have a peg upon which to hang his manifold views and opinions. The theatre, when I am not writing directly of it, serves me as such a peg. For thirty years I have discussed, in terms more or less related to the theatre and often in terms so distantly related to it that it was hardly discernible, everything from the marriage and burial ceremonies of the Hottentots to the remarkably improved grade of beer brewed at Metz. It is simply a dramatic critic's misfortune that once he becomes known, even in his earliest days, as a dramatic critic, no one will ever regard him as anything but a dramatic critic, even though he may write a dozen books with no barest mention of the drama in them, commit bigamy, or do anything else to differentiate and distinguish himself. A literary critic may write literary criticism until he is ninety, and no one will ask him how he can stand having ploughed through so many books. But let a dramatic critic remain even so little as five years in harness, and a great wonderment, dubiety and speculation set in. Yet, with one or two exceptions, what writings on the theatre and drama have lived? Those of men who knew the theatre and drama only a short while and then retired from all contact with them, or those of men to whom the theatre and drama were part and parcel of their life's considerable and consistent interest?

20

At the beginning of each new season we engage the traditional yowls against what incompetents who have suffered from it dub destructive criticism. About such so-called destructive criticism tons of white paper have been inked pro and con. A favorite argument con is that the destructive critic is altogether too greatly inclined to be personal. To this, Shaw, it seems to me, has made the best retort. " The artist," he says, " who accounts for my disparagement by alleging personal animosity on my part is quite right. When people do less than their best, and do that less at once badly and self-complacently, I hate them, loathe them, detest them, long to tear them limb from limb and strew them in goblets about the stage or platform." "The true critic," he concludes, "is the man who becomes your personal enemy on the sole provocation of a bad performance, and will only be appeased by good performances."

But it occurs to me that what the howlers against this so-called destructive criticism most greatly object to, although they may not be aware of the fact, is not so much destructive criticism *per se* as the frequent manner of its expression. Destructive criticism embroidered with polite literary graces and circumlocutions arouses small wrath on the part of the victim. But destructive criticism that has done with evasion and says its say simply, bluntly, and directly to the point, without verbal hypocrisy or other folderol, is like an adder. Both may at bottom say exactly the same thing, yet it is the latter that is at the root of all the complaint. If Henry James and Shaw were both to have written a criticism of the same worthless play and were to have said exactly the same offensive things against it, it would have been Shaw's criticism that would have been declared destructive by the toasted author. James' — though, as I have said, it expressed exactly the same thoughts — would have avoided the indignation of the author by virtue of its literary convolutions and chaste flourishes. We engage in active practice today critics of both the Shavian and Jamesian schools of expression. Their basic critical attitudes are often identical. But it is the former who, because of their simple literary directness and straight-from-the-shoulder expression, suffer the stigma of being mere blasters instead of architects.

Let us experiment with a couple of examples. Among the musical comedies and farces produced in the New York theatre not so long ago were Fred Stone's " Smiling Faces " and Hans Kottow's " The Stork Is Dead." Neither was worth the ink to blow it up; both were, from any point of view, completely meritless and completely without even a commonplace entertainment value. So much agreed upon, there were two critical ways to approach them. In the case of the Stone exhibit, one was as follows: " Fred Stone revealed himself as a sadly outdated comedian whose comedy methods belong to the dead Nineties; the show in which he proved a dismal bore belonged similarly to the dead Nineties and was an even more terrible bore than he; and the company supporting him was made up, among others, of an ingénue with legs like Grant's Tomb, an English juvenile who after speaking his each line turned his face to the audience and delivered himself of a self-congratulatory toothful grin, and a female clown whose humors were confined to a weight of two hundred pounds." The second way was as follows: " Mr. Stone's comedic technique, one firmly grounded in the gala tradition of the gay and glamorous Nineties, is still what it always was; amidst the theatre's mutations he has remained steadfast and faithful in his methods, having no traffic with these more modern zanies; the show to which he vouchsafed his memorable pranks was equally a bit of rosemary of the period that remains wistful in the recollection of the older theatregoer; and the company supporting him was made up, among others, of an ingénue whose limbs had all the lovely contours of Borghese — aye, Mithridates — vases, an English juvenile who after speaking his each line did not, as do so many juveniles, hide his handsome face from the audience but rather allowed the latter to share with him his own seduction by turning it to us and enhancing its fascination with a proud, broad smile that revealed all his fine teeth, and a comédienne whose comedic virtuosity, were such things to be measured so, might have been estimated as being seven times as notable as that of a comédienne seven stones less impressive in conspicuity."

I submit the two ways to the adjudication of those who desire simple critical facts as quickly as possible.

In the case of " The Stork Is Dead," there were similarly two approaches on the part of destructive criticism. The first consisted in something like this, duly expanded and elaborated upon: " For those who are loyal in their admiration for Hungarian paraphrases of the old Palais Royal farces, be the paraphrases good or bad, this farce may retain some nostalgic interest, particularly in the instance of those devotees who, impatient with the more subtle and complex drolleries of modern farce, find unalloyed amusement in a forthright and courageous insistence, voiced at intervals of every five minutes, upon the exotic fact that child-birth is less a result of an ornithological phenomenon than of a biological." The second consisted in this: " ' The Stork Is Dead ' is cheap, smutty hogwash."

21

A favorite retort to the critic when he finds fault with a play is, if he doesn't like it, why didn't he write a better one himself. Contrary to the critic's usual lofty disdain of what he pleases himself to regard as a mere sample of vaudeville facetia, there is something in the challenge. It sometimes happens, of course, that the critic is kept so busy with his job reviewing bad plays that he hasn't the time to write the better ones demanded of him. But, nevertheless, he should have enough time occasionally to tell the writers of the bad plays how he would have written them and made of them, perhaps, something better than they are.

Confronted, for example, by a poor play like Mr. Sidney Howard's " Alien Corn," the critic should not experience much difficulty in pointing out to Mr. Howard how he would have improved upon it by spraying its theme with a measure of observational intelligence. That theme, you may recall, concerns a young woman pianist of Viennese blood, who, set down among the people of a small college town in the American Middle West, finds the air stifling to artistic temperament, finds, too, a comprehensive lack of sympathy and understanding and encouragement, and packs off in despair to Vienna, there presumably to find in turn everything that has been missing to her and her work. What we have here, obviously, is the plainest and stalest theatrical hokum: the theory, so intently fondled by the Harvard boys among our playwrights, that the American atmosphere — and that in the Middle West particularly — is suffocating to artistic enterprise and that, contrastedly, Europe is just so much grand oxygen.

As anyone with half an eye's experience or with a measure of playwriting imagination should appreciate, American patronage and encouragement of artists — especially completely bogus ones — are often so excessive (in certain sections of the Middle West particularly) that the situation skirts the coasts of burlesque. The pushing Babbittry and its wives, the new-rich of cities and small towns, the culture-seekers and the society-seekers, all strain to identify themselves with the arts and their practitioners. Any player of chop-sticks, provided only he have a name that sounds vaguely Polack, fingers six inches long and hair sixteen, returns from the Middle West with his digestive tract and kidneys completely ruined by the over-enthusiasms of hospitality. In Vienna, the fellow would have to buy even his own coffee. So, rewriting Mr. Howard's play, the critic would bequeath to it both novelty and honesty, and some modern intelligence, by deleting all of its present sentimental fraudulence and bringing the young woman pianist from present-day Vienna, which is as dead as a door-nail so far as any kind of artistic encouragement and sympathy goes and where she had found her-self stifled, into the sympathy and encouragement of the little American Babbitt college town. That, too, might be hokum of a sort, one admits, but at any rate it would not wear the beard of the Howard brand.

Miss Susan Glaspell's "The Comic Artist," another poor play, deals with an artist who, now married, encounters the young woman with whom he once had an affair in Paris and is again drawn sexually to her, the resulting fermentation — negotiated in a barn — bringing tragic misery to his patient wife, to himself, to the young woman and to the latter's spouse, his brother. All this, the author — despite the calendar hint that we are living in the 1930's — handles with an Ibsenish gravity. While it is apparent that the theme is more properly, in this day, suited to farce or light comedy, I shall not make the point, as it has come to be a cliché of criticism that takes the easiest way out of such matters. Let us therefore, for the moment, concur in Miss Glaspell's notion that her theme must be treated with a straight face. How then to illuminate it?

The character of the artist's wife, as drawn by Miss Glaspell, is a more or less understanding woman, no longer young and silly. One would accordingly have re-written the last act and, while allowing some natural indignation to remain the portion of the betrayed young woman's husband (the artist's younger brother), would have brought the artist's wife to chuckle quietly over her own husband's supreme idiocy in allowing himself to be dragged into the inevitable disillusion of a resumed old affair, particularly, and above all, one that had had Paris as its origin. His own moral qualms, contrition and disappointment would only add fuel to her laughter and, on that laughter, now loud and philosophically merry, the curtain would come down. All this would fail to make the play a good one, true, but it would make it a slightly less outmoded and dull one than it presently is.

In " We, the People," Elmer Rice confected a propaganda diatribe against various phases of American injustice. It failed of all conviction because its examples and propaganda were uniformly and unremittingly of the hit-'em-in-the-jaw school. If, bribed with a sufficient number of authentic beers, the critic had been wheedled into writing the same basic play, he would have made it infinitely more convincing and effective by completely reversing the propaganda scheme, that is, by ironically arguing the absurdity of the charges of injustice, the full truth of which would at all times thus be doubly apparent to and impressed upon the auditors. Even a sardonic *compère,* added to Mr. Rice's play as it stands and made to interrupt the indignant action at intervals with good-natured and suavely humorous defences of capitalism, would, without damaging its thesis in the slightest, remove the overdose of rancor from it and help it immeasurably.

A final example: the play called " Men Must Fight," by the Messrs. Lauren and Lawrence. The theme here was Edition No. 27 of Galsworthy's " The Mob " and of the various other plays, fore and aft, contending that, for all a man's belief in pacifism, the waving of flags and rattle of war drums will upset and heat him to the point of putting on a uniform and rushing off to fight. The authors' coda consisted in the distaff argument that the only way to stop men's nonsense in this direction was for women to refuse to have any more male babies (the authors apparently being privy to some new scientific method for predetermining sex). Although the play was greeted as something very recherché by many of the critics who in their excitement evidently forgot all about Galsworthy, Lysistrata, *et al.,* it occurs to one of their number that a relatively newer and more entertaining play might have been fashioned out of the idea of men of various ages who have fought in various wars, who have learned their single lesson and who, when the drums sound again the call to battle, rush up to the attic, jump into their old uniforms, hurry back to the windows downstairs, and give the brave boys marching proudly past to the thrilling strains of a half dozen national anthems one joint, vociferous, fervid and very elegant raspberry.

22

Any sound dramatic critic must periodically be guilty of vulgarity and bad manners. (In which respect he is not so very different from Ben Jonson, General Grant, and St. Paul.) There are occasions in the critical life when bad manners are an absolute necessity. If a playwright (or some person who has the presumption to imagine himself one) insults invited critical attention by hitting it in the face with a contemptible and overly odoriferous cheese-pie, it is pretty hard to figure out why he should not be hit in the face, in turn, with an even larger and juicier critical equivalent. The critic who meets excessively bad manners in such artistic directions with good manners may be a gentleman, but he is a damned weak, ineffective, and un-read critic. Good manners are for press-agents. Bad manners are the privilege of any critic who is properly out-raged and disgusted by all forms of artistic, intellectual and emotional bounderism.

23

Certain of the plays that the critics of today sneer at are precisely the sort that the selfsame critics fifteen years ago would have declared significant contributions to the American drama, which they would not have been then any more than they are now. If you will take the trouble to look back into the files of yesterday's criticism, you will find that plays exactly like these presently sneered-at ones — bad plays all — were heartily endorsed as more or less profound contributions to the native drama simply and solely on the ground that, irrespective of any intrinsic merit, they approached their subject matter with what was at the time an independent and theatrically unfash-ionable point of view. Much of the currently ridiculed trash is exactly the kind of trash that the critical professors who now laugh at it were wont not so long ago to include in their austere collections of " Representative American Plays."

24

A young man, suffering from an ambition to go to the theatre every night and thus accelerate what was already a recognizable case of incipient dementia, some months since inquired of me what I held to be the first rule for a dramatic critic to follow. " Never read dramatic criticism! " I told him. The reading of such criticism, I elaborated, having already driven most playwrights, actors, producers and critics crazy, would prove doubly dangerous in the instance of a young man like himself who showed signs of being crazy even before he began.

How anyone in any way connected with the theatre can read much of current dramatic criticism and retain his mental balance, I do not know. More than anything else, in point of fact, has the reading of other critics' criticism — even that of the more estimable — been responsible for the increasing derangement of dramatic critics themselves, so widely observable, and the increasing vertigo of their craft. The critic who reads criticism, like the bartender who drinks his own stuff, is doomed. To retain his legs and preserve the color of his nose, he must be a total abstainer.

To prove this to my young friend, I bade him go forth and fetch back with him a number of the first daily and monthly journals he could lay his hands on. Upon his return, I asked him to open the one on top and read what he found therein. It was an English gazette (*The Tatler*) and from the critical pages of Mr. James Agate, one of the ablest of the London dramatic critics, he read the following: " Ronald Mackenzie's ' Musical Chairs' is the best first play written in forty years. . . . Eugene O'Neill's ' Strange Interlude' is a colossal piece of pretentious bunk." " Do you happen to have seen those two plays? " I asked him. " Yes, sir," he answered, sufficiently.

The next journal was the New York *Sun* and from the pages of its dramatic critic, in a review of Rachel Crothers' " When Ladies Meet," my young friend read the following: " The women are understood, and set down, with a comprehension few among our playwrights are likely to equal. The men — well, it seems to us that Miss Crothers has once again come a cropper with one of her men, and that she weakens her last act — and psychologically her whole play — by it. She makes so poor a fish out of the man both women love that it is hard to imagine either of them loving him." " How," I asked my young friend, " if, as the critic insists, Miss Crothers understands and sets down women with a comprehension few among our playwrights are likely to equal, is it hard for the critic to imagine two of Miss Crothers' women characters loving the poor fish? " " I don't know, sir," he replied, sufficiently.

The next journal was the *Nation* and in the pages of

its critic, the very intelligent and sagacious Mr. Joseph Wood Krutch, from a review of "Mademoiselle," my young friend read the following: "Its author, the Frenchman Jacques Deval, may be remembered as the man responsible for 'Her Cardboard Lover' . . . but the new play reveals him in the much softer mood appropriate to the slightly maudlin story of a frozen-faced governess." "Do you happen to know Jacques Deval's play as it was in France, before Miss Grace George adapted the ironic Deval into a 'softer mood' and his play into the 'slightly maudlin' story?" I asked my young friend. "Yes, sir," he answered, sufficiently.

The next journal was the since defunct *Bookman*. In its pages, my young friend read, from a critical article on the O'Neill drama by one Kemelman, the following: "I would merely point out that the tom-tom in 'The Emperor Jones,' although a new device, produced no change in the established technique of the drama. The use of the tom-tom is a trick whose only virtue is its novelty; it cannot be used again and it has not been used since." "As to the 'new device,'" I inquired of my young friend, "do you recall a similar use of the tom-tom, years before, in Austin Strong's 'The Drums of Oude,' Conan Doyle's 'Fires of Fate,' and other such plays?" "Yes, sir, my father has spoken of it to me," he answered. "And as to 'it cannot be used again and it has not been used since,'" I asked him, "have you yourself not seen any number of plays like 'Gold Braid,' 'Heat Wave,' *et al.,* to say nothing of such dramatic sound paraphrases as 'Distant Drums,' and to say nothing, of course, of a score or more of talking pictures?'" "Yes, sir," he replied, sufficiently.

Turning again to the *Bookman,* my young friend read further: "In 'Strange Interlude' O'Neill uses another type of label, the aside. . . . In other words, the audience is treated to a series of explanatory notes on the emotions of the characters in the play. It is a confession on the part of the playwright that he cannot express himself in the dramatist's medium." "Wasn't it similarly a confession on the part of Shakespeare that he could not express himself in the dramatist's medium?" I asked my young friend. "Yes, sir," he answered.

The next journal was the New York *Herald Tribune,* two copies of it. From a review of the Abbey Theatre Players' repertoire, in the pages of Mr. Richard Watts, my young friend read the following: "As if in protest against the popular belief that their fellow countrymen are a merry and heedless people, given exclusively to whimsicality and high spirits, the Celt dramatists seem currently bent on dramatizing the essential melancholia of their race, on delving into the cruelty and intolerance they find in Irish life, on pillorying themselves for their sins and their follies. The modern Irish dramatist is as melancholy as Hamlet, as self-scourging as a pre-Bolshevik Russian." "Just what about any popular belief that the Irish are a merry and heedless people, given exclusively to whimsicality and high spirits?" I asked my young friend. "I don't seem to have heard of it, sir," he replied. "And are such modern estimable Celt dramatists as Brinsley Macnamara, George Shiels, Lady Gregory, George Birmingham, Lord Dunsany, George Fitzmaurice, Denis Johnston and Lennox Robinson bent ever on dramatizing the essential melancholia of their race, on delving into the cruelty and intolerance they find in Irish life, on pillorying themselves for their sins and their follies?" I continued. "I haven't noticed it," he answered.

Again my young friend turned to the same journal and from it read the following: "The Irish are generally thought of as a hyper-sensitive race, whose feelings are so easily injured that a play unflattering to their sensibilities will drive them into wild outbursts of indignation . . . yet the O'Casey tragedy ('Juno and the Paycock') scourges its people with savage intensity and assails the frailties of Gaelic character with merciless contempt. Whatever you may say about the Irish, they can certainly stand self-criticism in their theatre." "What about the merry hell the Irish have raised on a dozen recent occasions in Dublin — *e.g.* 'The Playboy of the Western World' and 'The Plough and the Stars' — when plays unflattering to their sensibilities have been produced? And what about de Valera's official condemnation of this very 'Juno and the Paycock,' along with 'The Plough and the Stars'?" I asked my young friend. "As you say, sir, what about it?"

The next journal was the New York *Times*. From

a criticism of an English version of " Yoshe Kalb " by my good brother, Mr. Brooks Atkinson, my young friend extracted this morsel: " Is this the fable that seemed so colorful when it was masked in Yiddish last year? It is. Furthermore, it seems to have been put into English with some feeling for rhythm; the translation is innocent of linguistic crime. But . . . it is diffuse and unimaginative. *English is not the language of wonder . . .*" " Really? " I ventured to my young friend. " Poor King James' Bible, poor Bard of Avon, poor Milton."

He did not reply.

I looked around to see what had become of him.

He was standing on his head in the corner, loudly singing chop-sticks and proclaiming that he was Demetrius Phalereus or Lola Montez, he couldn't decide which.

" You're drunk. Where did you get that beer? " I asked, observing the foam on his mouth.

" That ain't beer," he answered. " And, by the way, wipe yours off."

25

The failure of so much of propaganda drama may be accounted for in the fact that drama is not for passion of belief, but for passion of feeling.

26

The leading critical argument against such an anti-Nazi propaganda play as Leslie Reade's " The Shattered

Lamp " is that its events are based so closely upon the news and are hence so familiar in advance to the audience that all suspense is lacking and the play is bound to be dull. Like many other critical arguments, I enjoy the traitorous honor of denouncing this particular one as so much jabber. If advance familiarity with the events of a play inevitably makes the play dull, Heaven help the theatrical business! It is, of course, true that plays based upon the news are already familiar to first-night critical audiences, but it is also true that plays not based upon the news are equally familiar to every other successive audience that is able to read the newspapers, weeklies and monthly magazines. It is an uncommon theatregoer who hasn't read the plot and development of the play he is seeing in the reviewers' columns and who doesn't know just as much in advance and doesn't suffer the same lack of suspense in the case of something like " The Shining Hour " or " Sailor, Beware! " as in the case of some news play like " The Shattered Lamp " or " They Shall Not Die." The great success of many dramatized best sellers — " Dodsworth " is a recent example — proves further that familiarity with the materials of a play never yet has diminished the customers' enjoyment or the box-office returns.

It isn't plot familiarity that counts; it is the internal effectiveness (or external actor effectiveness) of the play itself that keeps the box-office boys either busy or at the ball game. Everybody knows how the Cinderella story comes out, but that hasn't hurt the stage Cinderella story time and time again. Just as a badly handled Cinderella play will fail, so will a badly handled play based upon the facts in the news. " The Shattered Lamp " was a badly handled job, and so it failed to interest anybody. If it had been a well-handled one, it might have succeeded, even if everybody in the audience could have recited it in full before the curtain went up. People do not go to the theatre to be surprised so much as they go to be satisfied. If the opposite were true, every fool mystery play — with the solution duly kept secret at the request of the producer by the gentlemanly reviewers — would make a million dollars.

27

It has always seemed to me to be ridiculous to expect a reviewer to chronicle just what happened in a song and dance show that he liked. If he can remember all that happened, you may rest assured he didn't enjoy the show as much as he tries to tell you in print that he did. The enjoyment of such shows is a completely transient thing. It consists in a series of gayly ingested moments that fade from the memory forthwith, as they properly should. The best song and dance show, accordingly, is like a prestidigitator's hand bewilderingly making things appear and disappear. What appeared and disappeared is not material to the memory; only the general idea of the prestidigitator himself is. Long and detailed reviews of girl and tune shows belie, as observed, the good time that their writers allege to have had at them.

28

One of the commonest delusions about play reviewers is that they are fond of consulting with one another between the acts or at the conclusion of an evening as to the merits of the play they have been reviewing. The delusion is shared, and enthusiastically, by many producers, playwrights and actors. Nothing could be more false. In the first place, the average reviewer is so enamoured of himself that he would not condescend even to listen to the opinion of any other reviewer. And, in the second place, three-fourths of the plays the reviewers are called to pass upon are such utter junk that conferring on their quality would be as superfluous as holding conferences on the health of the stiffs in the morgue.

29

No sooner had last season got under way than we observed a number of plays, at best deserving of faint praise, touted by the critical gentry as something eminently and magnificently lush. To believe that there was anything in the least dishonest or hypocritical in the appraisals is to be grievously mistaken, for, by and large, the present-day reviewer is a sincere, upright, and wholly unprejudiced fellow — a very different one from his brother of fifteen and twenty years ago. I desire to emphasize the point, since the deduction I wish to make from it might otherwise be taken by some to be a reflection upon the local critical probity. The deduction is as follows:

While the overly enthusiastic reviews that are presently being accorded certain very dubious plays are in themselves completely honest and the scrupulous and undissembling refraction of their sponsors' critical convictions, there undoubtedly yet remains a reason behind the reason for them. That reason is an understandable one, and is twofold. For some time now, the professional theatrical critics have foolishly been made to feel — and have foolishly felt — that, unless something was done about it pretty soon, the theatre, which is their source of livelihood, would die of celluloid poisoning.

Massaging themselves into the plerophory that there must be *something* in the cocksure statements of the various movie executives (themselves mostly in the bankruptcy courts) that the movies were rapidly driving the theatre into the discard; alarmedly reading the published affidavits of the larger movie cathedrals that they were playing to a gross of sixty and seventy thousand dollars weekly (showing a net weekly loss on investment of twenty thousand); giving a trusting ear to the pronunciamentos of various producers (who had lost all their money in the stock market) that the theatre was too dangerous an institution longer to risk their money in — the critics very truthfully, if very innocently, began to believe that they were part and parcel of the situation's salvation. It was

[29]

not always a consciously arrived at belief — far from it — but, consciously or unconsciously, it was, down in their innards, a belief none the less.

Like an absinthe drip in a summer's twilight, the conviction gradually permeated their very souls, and a kind of boozy good-will, a hot wish to believe, a species of critical rosiness, began to steal over them. "We'll show those movies where they get off!" sounded, subconsciously, the little whispering voice within them. "We'll tell the world the theatre is a long way from being dead, or even sick!" repeated the little hidden voice. And so, almost without their realizing it, there was born in them a critical philanthropy of such proportions that, were they soberly and surgically to meditate it, they themselves would be the first just a little aghast and struck all of a heap to perceive it.

Danger lies in such a critical disposition. For it is ever a way with criticism to support its individual position by persistently asserting the verity of its initial opinion and never admitting that there may have been a flaw in it. Successful criticism is the convincing reiteration of beliefs that may often be dubious. It thus comes about that what was initially merely a relative judgment — criticism based solely on comparative values — is gradually transformed, by way of a defense mechanism, a critical protective coloration, or maybe a kind of personal vanity, into part of a body of critical doctrine. Or, in any event, into something that the critic himself persuades himself is a forthright and sound conclusion. . . . Critical praise unjustified is bread cast upon the waters; it returns to the critic in time as an embarrassing and corrupting whole delicatessen store.

It is the furious wish and will to have plays good that is currently often playing havoc with sound critical standards. And not only to have plays good but to have the players good. We are thus entertained, as I have noted, by a third-rate melodrama like "Double Door" hailed as first-rate stuff simply because it isn't sixth-rate and, to boot, is acted on an ominously darkened stage and directed as if it had been written by Calvin Coolidge. We thus hear extolled as very fine dramatic art a play like "Men in White" which, while not without dignity of intention and one or two effective theatrical scenes, is little more than second-rate Brieux. We thus observe a crude, if periodically amusing, little farce-comedy like "Sailor, Beware!" stampeded into a box-office rodeo, for all the world as if the combined comic genius of Goldoni, Molière and Senator Couzens had gone into it. And, in the quarter of histrionism, we behold that fine singer but laughably inferior actor, that colored Johnny Weissmuller, that licorice Walter Hampden, Mr. Paul Robeson, garlanded with blooms as a bigger and better Salvini, while out of the corner of another eye we discern that nice little girl, Miss Francesca Bruning, critically panegyrized as the heavenly feminine and wistfully nostalgic ghostess of Mary Anderson, Maude Adams and Bonnie Maginn simply because, in "Amourette," she had on an old-fashioned long soft white ruffled petticoat.

30

There was a day, and not so very long ago, when any musical show, however excellent, was looked down upon as something just a bit critically undignified, and worthy only of the attention of the second-string reviewer, the first-string professor dedicating his career rather to the genuine art works of Charles Klein, Augustus Thomas and Eugene Walter. All such nonsense is now fortunately a thing of the past, safely buried in the grave along with William Winter, J. Ranken Towse and the Columbia University hazlitts (excepting Brander Matthews, who had sense enough to appreciate that one pretty girl's beautiful leg was worth all the plays that Alfred Sutro ever wrote, particularly when it was lifted into the air).

31

In some earlier period and in some inscrutable manner there was born a critical legend to the effect that dramatizations of novels are seldom satisfactory and are usually doomed to failure. It has been a legend of considerable persistence to this day. Yet like many other critical legends, including the belief that a French play always and inevitably must lose something in translation (what of " The Captive," for example, or of " The Three Daughters of M. Dupont," or of " Pasteur "?), it is notable for its

[32]

hollowness. It is true that certain dramatizations are and have been as little satisfactory to the critics as to the general public; and it is equally true that the stage version of a novel must necessarily omit certain elements valuable to the novel form that are valueless to the dramatic, and so disappoint the playgoer who remains, in his theatre seat, refractorily a reader. But a careful survey of the American theatre reveals the fact that not only have dramatizations of novels been as close to the taste of its public as a like proportion of original plays, but that, in addition, they have figured among the most uncommonly prosperous of all theatrical ventures. And what is more, a considerable number of them have apparently been as acceptable to the critics as to the laymen.

It would be possible to take up several pages in incontrovertible statistical proof, but I merely suggest the general outline of that proof by recalling dramatizations of novels — all successful and many of them endorsed by the critics of their day — ranging from " East Lynne " to " Uncle Tom's Cabin," " Dr. Jekyll and Mr. Hyde " to " Salomy Jane," " Little Lord Fauntleroy " to " Becky Sharp," " Camille " to " The Honor of the Family," " Sapho " to " Sweet Kitty Bellairs," " The Corsican Brothers " to " When Knighthood Was In Flower," " Ben Hur " to " Trilby," and " Monte Cristo " to " Rip Van Winkle." Many of these, it will be recognized, made great fortunes. What, too, of " The Prisoner of Zenda," of " The Christian," of " Raffles," of " Under Two Flags," of " The

Three Musketeers," of "Sherlock Holmes," of "The Little Minister," of "The Great Adventure," of "Monsieur Beaucaire," of "The Trail of the Lonesome Pine," of "Seventeen," and of "Treasure Island"? And what, to come a bit closer to the present, of "The Bat," "The Masquerader," "The Green Hat," "The Age of Innocence," "Payment Deferred," "Rain," "Alice in Wonderland," "Tobacco Road," and "Dodsworth"? For every failure like "Thunder on the Left," or "Elmer Gantry," or any other such poorly dramatized novel (the fault not of the critical theory of dramatization but of the dramatizer) you will find a success. And probably two.

32

Answering such persons as have indulgently smiled away his affair with Ellen Terry, Shaw has written: "Let those who may complain that it was all on paper remember that only on paper has humanity yet achieved glory, beauty, truth, knowledge, virtue and abiding love." A thought, in coincidence, presents itself. Of all friends among men that a woman may possess, a writer is perhaps the most greatly to be treasured. Perhaps not always in his personal capacity, but assuredly in his professional. Consider the case history of women's glory and of women's loveliness and of women's fame — and reflect on the pens of men that sang behind them. What would Louise Colet have been — who ever, indeed, would so much as have heard of her — if it had not been for Flaubert; and what of du Châtelet without Voltaire, and of Madame Hansa without Balzac? Think of Elizabeth Barrett without a Browning, of Madame du Deffand without a Horace Walpole. Would Duse still live today had there been no d'Annunzio — even no Arthur Symons? George Sand was a monstrosity until de Musset made her something of an angel. As Dumas invented Sarah Bernhardt, Shaw invented for the memory of coming generations not only his Ellen Terry but Mrs. Patrick Campbell — as the younger Guitry invented, out of nothing, the realistically imaginary Yvonne Printemps. Without D. H. Lawrence, the Mesdames Dodge-Luhan, Carswell and Co. would still be publicly unborn. Where but on paper live Joan of Arc, and Florence Nightingale, and Edith Cavell? . . . The Mona Lisa herself would be overlooked in the dull dust of the years had it not been for Walter Pater.

33

In the seventy years of his life, he produced a succession of fine and worthy books. In his seventy-first year, failing in strength and tired, he produced something negligible. "Hum," derisively proclaimed the critics, "a sky-rocket!"

CHAPTER II

The American Theatre Today

ↄ   ↄ

The historian of the American theatre must recognize that it is today "news" on two grounds: first, because it has changed completely from what it previously has been, and, second, because with the change there has come about a coincidental very great change in the character of its audience and its drama. The American theatre, up to even so recently as six or seven years ago, was a hybrid institution, appealing in part to the casual moviegoer as well as to the more definite theatregoer. Its dramatic fare was generally such as to satisfy — or at least to attempt to satisfy — the tastes of both, equally and simultaneously. The result more often than not, accordingly, was the inevitable one of trying to sit on two stools. Neither the moviegoer nor, more importantly, the theatregoer was propitiated.

The consequence was soon, and alarmingly, evident. The moviegoer who had been in the habit of attending the theatre intermittently gave up the theatre entirely. And the theatregoer, hitherto in the habit of attending the theatre more regularly, gave it up to a considerable degree. There came about, naturally, a collapse of the theatre business, the statistics of which are already sufficiently and grievously known.

In this juncture, the theatre in various of its component parts — managers, producers, dramatists, actors — necessarily had to take stock of itself. Was it to die, or was it to live? And out of this stock-taking there was born the new theatre — or at least the *beginnings* of the new theatre — together with the new audience and the new drama.

What is this new-born theatre? It is a theatre that has had imposed upon it the necessity of abandoning in major part what may be termed the fifty-fifty drama, that is, the drama designed to appeal to the half-movie-minded, half-drama-minded audience, and the equal necessity of sponsoring at least some faint approximation to what may be called the hundred per cent drama, that is, drama that shall appeal to the relatively superior emotions and relatively superior intelligence of the simon-pure theatregoer. That plays are still produced from time to time which are subsequently purchased by the motion picture people for film purposes has no other significance than the motion picture people's belief that fifty-fifty motion pictures (half movie-half drama) will appeal equally to moviegoers and theatregoers, and hence draw a portion of the latter into the screen parlors. The motion picture people will undoubtedly learn their sad lesson in due time just as in the analogous direction the theatre learned its sad lesson.

The theatre has realized that it can no longer offer its customers, at two or three dollars a head, the kind of drama that they can obtain in the film houses for from thirty to fifty-five cents. The motion picture people will come to realize that a mere second-hand repetition of theatre drama at any price will not long satisfy customers of an entertainment medium that depends, above everything else, upon surprise, shock and novelty. It is as commercially foolish to show theatre drama in film houses as it would be to show films in dramatic theatres. For what makes big money in the film houses has been demonstrated in the general run to be either stories written directly for the screen or plays brought over from the theatre and so altered for screen purposes as to be barely recognizable.

Having regained its birthright — not without a hard struggle with itself — the theatre has set about considering just what has happened to it. It has found, first, that it now has an audience, still decidedly limited, that must be met on terms quite different from the heterogeneous, larger audience of yesterday; second, that its drama, to be successful with that audience, must be a drama different from the drama of yesterday; and third, that it has already partly begun not only to meet the new audience on the required terms but that it has also evolved, at least in a measure, the drama that is other than the drama of yesterday.

The new theatre audience is a particularized audience, or, in the vulgar expression, a "class" audience. It is an audience that has guaranteed the success of such dramas as " Strange Interlude " and " Mourning Becomes Electra," the mere excessive length of which would unquestionably have foredoomed them to failure with the mixed and impatient theatre audience of past years. It is an audience that has utterly no use for the smut so favored by the old mixed audience, as witness the overnight failure of such recent filth as " The Stork Is Dead," " Love and Babies," " The Great Magoo," and " It Pays To Sin." It is an audience that demands of a dramatist that he no longer condescend to it in the slightest degree, but meet it on its own intelligent and experienced emotional level.

By virtue of this demand, there has come over our theatre drama such a forced metamorphosis as, some years ago, would hardly have been dreamed possible, even by the most optimistic critic. These years ago, the three cardinal articles in the catalogue of successful dramatic hokum were Mother, the Baby, and the Flag. Today they are guarantees of ridicule and failure. Let a playwright attempt to coax an audience's sympathetic reaction with any one of them, or even with all three rolled together, and the neighing of the horses attached to the storehouse wagons outside will drown out the audience's ribald laughter. Mother in the new drama is no longer the silver-haired angel she arbitrarily always was in the old drama; she is a human being with all a human being's faults as well as virtues. Baby is no longer invariably a little bundle of sugar; baby is often just a plain out-and-out brat. And as for the Flag, even its hitherto uniformly successful capitalizer, Mr. George M. Cohan, has been derided out of waving it.

The new drama, whatever its deficiencies, is and must be an honest drama: honest with its audience and honest with itself. Consider, for example, the matter of what have been known antecedently in the theatre as " sympathetic " characters. Up to very recent years, one of the main demands made of a dramatist was that he make his central male or female figure a sympathetic person, that is, that the attributes and conduct of the character be such as to gain the respect, affection, commiseration and *rapprochement* of the audience. The demand was such an imperative and arbitrary one that, in the whole history of successful American box-office drama, there was not a single play that violated the injunction. In only one such play in that history, indeed, was there even a minor character not " sympathetic " that momentarily contrived to gain the sympathy of an audience, the character in point figuring in the Armstrong-Mizner play, " The Deep Purple," and acted, incidentally and significantly, by the late Jameson Lee Finney, an actor personally very popular with the audiences of his day. With the great audience change that has come about, intelligence, truth and honesty in character portrayal are insisted upon, let " sympathy " go where it may. What the new audience wants is not necessarily sympathetic characters but veracious characters. As a consequence, some of the plays most highly endorsed in the theatre today are plays with central characters that would have been hissed out of the theatre in other years.

Under the new dispensation, in point of fact, most of the old dramatic rules for success are passing into the discard. Even " suspense," a quality without which no play could achieve box-office success ten years ago, is no longer absolutely vital to prosperity with the new sophisticated audience, as witness, for instance, " Green Pastures." The mere quality of suspense, that is, nervous anticipation and anxiety as to succeeding dramatic events, has been dismissed as an absolute dramatic necessity. So with the majority of the other old rules and regulations. There is probably not one of them that cannot profitably be broken.

The new audience does not give a hoot for the so-called happy ending *per se*. It demands, instead, a logical ending uncorrupted by sentimentality. It has no longer any prejudice as to dramatic themes; any theme under the sun will be accepted by it if it be ably treated by the dramatist. Some years ago, the theatre insisted that a clergyman be presented always as a more or less noble creature; nowadays, he may be presented in any light consistent with realism. Formerly, the handling of religious and racial themes had to be negotiated with extreme tact; today any forthright handling is tolerated, so long as it be honest. " Touchy " subjects, that is, subjects dealing with certain abnormalities of mankind, were once taboo; now they are anything but " touchy," just so long as they are competently treated. Consider, for example, the success of

[41]

" The Green Bay Tree." Consider, as well, Mr. Priestley's "Dangerous Corner," which ran for half a season last year and which contained a character and scenes which, in the theatre's immediate yesterday, would have inflamed an audience's moral ire. The great success of a play like Mr. Coward's "Design For Living" would have been an utter impossibility ten years ago.

Consider, further, the manner in which the new attitude of audiences has affected even actors and actresses. Not many years ago, any popular woman star knew that she would sacrifice her popularity if she confessed to a sufficient age to show herself in a rôle which presented her as the mother of grown children. Still believing, indeed, that the theatre audience was the same old audience of their earlier days, several of the most conspicuous women stars a few seasons back peremptorily rejected the idea of playing the leading rôle in Mr. St. John Ervine's " The First Mrs. Fraser," on the ground that they did not dare risk losing their audiences' affection by appearing as maters of relatively advanced age. Among these actresses were Miss Ethel Barrymore and Miss Laurette Taylor. Miss Grace George, with considerably more sagacity as to the education of even the new popular taste, then undertook the rôle and scored one of the biggest theatre successes of her career. It is safe to venture that in the future neither Miss Barrymore nor Miss Taylor — nor any other mature woman star — will longer doubt that there is a new and greatly altered audience in the American theatre. The day of merely " pretty " rôles is done. A favorite actress is no longer a favorite simply on the ground of theatrical glamour and illusion; if she is to retain her favor, there must be, above all else, artistic bravery in her, and honesty as to the rôles she plays, and evidence of advancement in her profession. Few of the kind of rôles that made actresses audience-pets in the time of Charles Frohman will today avail an actress who desires to keep her hold on the new audience.

Gone, too, is the cigarette-picture ingénue — gone, doubtless, for good. The young woman who chooses the stage for a career must nowadays be much more than a sweet and cunning young thing; she must give evidence of acting talent. A glance at the younger women on the stage at the present time, along with a reflection on the general run of ingénues in other years, clearly illustrates the difference in audience predilection. In these young women one finds, aside from any personal comeliness, traces of real ability.

The new, intelligent audience, further still, is dramatically shock-proof. You cannot shock intelligence in the theatre, you can only disgust it. Thus, when some throw-back of a producer seeks to shock it with some cheap example of so-called " daring " drama — and through the shock capitalize the box-office — he succeeds only either in affronting it or putting it to sleep. Not a single play of this species produced in the theatre in the last half dozen years has drawn enough trade to keep it alive. With the better grade of so-called daring drama, intelligent interest has supplemented the older sensational interest. "The Captive," which was censored off the stage, due to audience protest in various quarters, a half dozen years ago, would unquestionably be unmolested by the present-day audience or by the authorities operating in its behalf. In the last two years, not one play has been censored by the authorities on moral grounds. The authorities, like the new audience, have also experienced a change in viewpoint and attitude. As a result, the theatre, being an honest theatre, is now a cleaner and more decent theatre. Where once it smirked and licked its lips, it now speaks the truth openly, and open truth is pretty generally clean.

The old American theatre, in short, is as dead as a door-nail. Its triviality, its hypocritical morals, its bastard audience and its obvious, gold-digging box-office are things of the past. The new American theatre, with all its ambitions and hopes, may true enough for all its great step forward be still far from the top of the celestial ladder, but it is climbing hard, and steadily, and unmistakably. And if ever it slips back, it will be done for.

We come now to a consideration of the economic side of the present-day theatre. That it is in a more healthful financial condition than it has been in some years is evident to even the casual observer. The reason for this, paradoxically enough, is the late depression, which turned out, so far as the theatre was concerned, to be a real blessing in disguise. In the first place, it put a stop to the idiotic building of new theatres, all so unnecessary as to be fore-doomed to failure. In the second place, it brought about the end of absurdly high theatre rentals, which frightened away even the bravest of experimental producers and the most eager producers of better-grade drama. In the third place, it brought about a reduction in the often exaggerated salaries of actors, and so further gave a better gambling chance of success to enterprising dramatic producers. In the fourth place, it cut the overhead in the business and mechanical departments. And in the fifth place, it gradually began to convert the theatre from a mad roulette wheel into something approximating a sound and legitimate business run on at least relatively sound and legitimate principles.

The great reduction in weekly theatrical rentals — in certain cases the reduction has amounted to as much as $3,500 on a previous $4,000 weekly rental — has, of course, attracted a proportion of fly-by-night and ignorant producers, with their fly-by-night and ignorant dramatic throwbacks to an earlier and meritless period of the theatre. But, with the new and higher audience demands, they have not lasted long and have largely been driven from the temple. The depression also eliminated the so-called theatre guarantee, that is, the necessity for an independent producer to guarantee the owner of a theatre a definite, fixed sum — usually very high — for a certain number of weeks and covering the lofty rental of the theatre. This system called severely upon the independent producer's available resources; it demanded of him a capital investment much greater than was logically reasonable; and it naturally induced in him, assuming that he was a fellow of decent dramatic aspiration and ideals, a measure of trepidation. And it was instrumental in making the production of the finer and often uncommercial drama a dangerous hazard. The result, in general, was a partiality on the part of independent producers to take a chance only with the kind of plays that seemed to have box-office possibilities. Real merit soon became a matter of diminished consideration.

With the greatly reduced rentals and the disappearance of the insisted-upon guarantee — sometimes demanded, in part, in a cash advance — the independent producer of standing has found the way cleared for the exercise of his dramatic ambitions. More, a good play, that may not get off any too well at the start, is now in a position to have some lease of life afforded to it, whereas in former days, if it did not pay at the very beginning, it was doomed to be closed, and instanter.

More important is the revivification of what is known in theatrical parlance as " the road," that is, the theatre outside of New York. Not only is there unmistakable evidence of a renewed hunger for the legitimate theatre in the thitherward cities, but even in the overgrown hamlets the inhabitants are displaying a keen appetite for the plays that, after these many years, are again occasionally coming their way. The tremendous success of " Green

Pastures " in the small towns of the South — which have always in the past been poor audience material — is a straw which shows the changed wind. Katharine Cornell, on a tour to the West Coast with " The Barretts of Wimpole Street," has played to standing-room-only business. George M. Cohan and O'Neill's " Ah, Wilderness! " have packed the road theatres. And towns and cities which for the last eight or ten years have turned a chilled shoulder to the legitimate stage in favor of the motion picture screen are beginning to return to their first, early love. The New York barometer indicates, as well, the changing barometers elsewhere.

CHAPTER III

The Good Old Days

Every so often, some elderly gentleman who has been connected with the theatre in one way or another, as a producer, actor, or perhaps merely inveterate playgoer, indites and has published a book. The said book, whoever and whatever its confectioner, exercises always the same *leit-motif,* to wit, the melancholy and drab aspect of the theatre world of the present as compared with the glamorous romance of that same world in the past. The most recent singer of the tune is Mr. George C. Tyler, the well-known impresario of other years, though by the time this appears it may well be that several other papas will have come forth with tomes that will, even so soon, post-date Mr. Tyler's. In view of the excess of propaganda in favor of these good old days, it may be meet to scrutinize the situation pro and con and determine just what is and what is not the truth concerning it. Being one who, though still able to get up out of bed in the mornings without the combined assistance of a nurse and a wall pulley, has experienced sufficient years to have lived through a portion of the aforesaid good old days, I take the liberty of offering my services toward the necessary enlightenment.

Going back twenty-five or thirty years — the period wistfully recollected by the majority of the sentimental bookmen — and comparing that magnificent epoch with the present, what do we find? First, let us consider the theatres themselves. To read the books, these theatres of the past were all so many gay and brilliant salons, filled nightly with unbelievably handsome ladies and swell cavaliers, the cream of the cream of fashion, literature, art, politics and the *beau monde,* whereas the theatres of today are all more or less frowzy dumps generally deserted or, on rare occasions, patronized exclusively by cloak and suit manufacturers, delicatessen dealers, moving picture scouts, Broadway dressmakers, smart-aleck dramatic critics, and other such riff-raff, no smallest element of which possesses either a soupçon of intelligence or a dress suit.

As I myself recall the picture, however, it doesn't seem to have looked at all like the one the moist-eyed literati wish us nostalgically to pine for. Of those invariably dazzling première audiences that they write of, I recollect, out of long and intimate experience, only one: the audience that attended the openings at Charles Frohman's Empire Theatre. And, even so, I can hardly see wherein lay the especially dazzling social and intellectual quality of such regular Empire first-nighters as Abe Hummel, Diamond Jim Brady, Jesse Lewisohn, Acton Davies,

Sandy Dingwall, Mannie Chappelle, George Kessler, André Bustanoby and Jackson Gouraud and his Aimée. As for the other opening night gatherings, I can — even with the prettiest strain of the imagination — remember none that was anything to write home and much less a book about. The mistake that the old boys have fallen into is that the audiences which they reminisce about contained friends of their earlier days, whom naturally they recall with affection and the subtle bacteria induced by the pathos of distance, whereas the audiences of today, however soundly and even brilliantly constituted, are made up of total strangers to them, about whom they personally know nothing. Yet I doubt if any one of the opening night audiences of the past over which they spill tender tears — the Empire alone hypothetically excepted — was in any reputable way up to the standard of the present-day opening night audience at the same Empire when Mr. Gilbert Miller is in charge, at the Martin Beck when Mr. Guthrie McClintic is in charge, at the New Amsterdam when Mr. Max Gordon is in charge, at the Plymouth when Mr. Arthur Hopkins is in charge, or at any one of a dozen other theatres when, irrespective of the management, a conspicuously meritorious playwright or actress or actor is on display. Furthermore, while the Theatre Guild openings may not be notable for their glamour, it is a safe bet that, when it comes to a matter of intelligence, they are considerably more notable than any three or four old Empire Theatre openings with their enchanting congresses of prominent wine-agents, shyster lawyers, and pleasantly alcoholized men-about-town.

So the theatres physically were also museums of warm and thrilling beauty, were they? Well, let us take a recollective look. I recall distinctly the old Garden Theatre, at the south-east corner of Madison Square Garden, where Colonel Henry W. Savage made some of his productions. Not only was it an excessively dirty showshop with green hangings that looked like crystallized Mills Hotel pea soup, but during the time a horse show, a dog show or the circus was in activity in the Garden itself, it enjoyed an empyreuma that was hardly an aid to the complete persuasiveness of romantic or sentimental drama. I recall, also, the Sire Brothers' Bijou, at Thirtieth Street and Broadway, where Nazimova made her first appearance in English in Owen Johnson's "The Comet," and you have my word for it that it was as desolate and thoroughly unattractive a little bandbox as ever masqueraded under the name of theatre. The famous Daly's, across the street on the same side of Broadway, had by this time — twenty-five and thirty years ago — also degenerated into a rat-trap and, though such stars as Julia Marlowe, William Faversham and others of equal eminence were playing there and though it was also there that Laurette Taylor was just beginning to make her reputation, the house was so badly lighted and its upholstery so dilapidated that the stage performances had a terrific tussle with the audience's patience, comfort and qualms as to the spotlessness of its frock and trouser seats. And the equally famous Wallack's directly across the way from the Bijou, where the hereinbefore mentioned Mr. Tyler made his productions, was in equally disreputable condition.

The old Madison Square Theatre, in West Twenty-fourth Street, let them try to fool you as they will, was in this period so run down that even the Minskys would have balked at it for a burlesque house. I recall having attended a certain opening night — the play was David Graham Phillips' one and only venture into drama — that was followed by no less than six different threats of suits against the management on the part of ladies whose gowns had been ruined by protruding nails, greasy chairs, and what not. The Princess, wherein Henry Miller introduced William Vaughn Moody to the public, situated on Broadway in the upper Twenties, was another black hole of Calcutta, and the Savoy, in West Thirty-fourth Street, in this era would have been a discredit physically to the smallest town on the Stair and Havlin circuit. As for the Majestic, in Columbus Circle, owing to the close proximity of Pabst's beer emporium on the downtown side, it was difficult for an audience to make up its combined mind and nose whether it was in a theatre or a brewery. Of all the theatres, indeed, there were just three and only three that could compare with any dozen or more in existence today. The three were the Empire, the Knickerbocker, and the Casino. When the New Amsterdam (not to mention the Lyceum and Globe) was subsequently built and flung its

Roxy peacocks to the night gaze, the public — used to the sordid and depressing theatres of the day — were as astounded and overcome as if in the presence of a miracle.

But, ah, those lovely, lovely girls of yesterday! Those great beauties of the stage twenty-five and thirty years ago! Those toasts of the town! Once again permit a gentleman of the old school who is still able to see without glasses politely to exclaim whatever is the belletristic equivalent of boloney. It isn't that I go so far as to say that there were no lovely girls in those days; there were a number, I well recall, who fluttered my then more youthful critical pen out of its accustomed poise and rationality. It is simply that a whole lot of the girls of that period who have been romanticized by the rosemary-boutonniered backward-lookers were the sort who, some years later, couldn't have got beyond Ziegfeld's outer office and, to-day, couldn't get nearer Hollywood than Berea, Ohio. Take, for example, the celebrated original "Florodora" sextette. To read the impassionable daddies, a member of the younger generation of the present day would imagine it to have been composed of such lulus as never before or since have been seen on this earth. The truth about it was that not one single girl in it was above even ordinary looks and that, some time later, it achieved its sole contribution of pulchritude when a vacancy in it was filled with a girl whom a member of the producing staff had seen scrubbing a brown-front door-step in East Twenty-sixth Street, *viz.*, Camille Clifford. The Mlle. Clifford was what the daddies like to remember all the other "Florodora" girls as having been.

Only in the case of "The Wild Rose" is there justification for the patriarchs' sentimental reflections. There were more really beautiful young women in that show than in all the others produced in those days put together, though — some years later — the Casino show called "Havana," with its remembered "Hello, People!" song, offered a sorority not wholly to be sniffed at. When Daly's, back in the late Nineties and early Nineteen Hundreds, played the Gaiety musical comedies, its stage now and again also disclosed a houri or two to stimulate the imagination — Vashti Earle for an example — but when the archæologists try to persuade you that every time you went to the theatre in those years you were literally knocked out of your seat by dramatic stages chock full of Maxine Elliotts, or even Gertrude Elliotts, and by music show choruses chock full of Bonnie Maginns, Lotta Fausts, Polly Chases, Edna Hunters, Irene Bentleys, May Naudains, May De Sousas and Eleanor Mayos, they are — to revert to a phrase of the time — pulling your leg. In the whole period under discussion, "The Wild Rose" alone excepted, there was not a music show stage that approached in feminine galvanism any one of the much later and more recent Ziegfeld stages or even George White stages.

We come to the plays. Let us take a particularly interesting season of twenty-five years ago and compare it with this very last season. In the season twenty-five years ago we find these outstanding dramatic exhibits: " The Awakening of Helena Ritchie," a dramatization of a novel of Margaret Deland's by Charlotte Thompson, " The Battle," by Cleveland Moffett, " The Barber of New Orleans," by Edward Childs Carpenter, " Blue Grass," by Paul Armstrong, " The Blue Mouse," an adaptation by Clyde Fitch, " The Call of the North," by George Broadhurst, " Father and the Boys," by George Ade, " The Fighting Hope," by William J. Hurlbut, " The Gentleman From Mississippi," by Thomas A. Wise and Harrison Rhodes, " Glorious Betsy," by Rida Johnson Young, " The House of a Thousand Candles," a dramatization of a Meredith Nicholson novel by George Middleton, " The Intruder," by Thompson Buchanan, " Jack Straw," by W. S. Maugham, " The Man From Home," by Booth Tarkington and Harry Leon Wilson, " The Melting Pot," by Israel Zangwill, " Myself, Bettina," by Rachel Crothers, " Paid in Full," by Eugene Walter, " Pierre of the Plains," by Edgar Selwyn, " The Royal Mounted," by Cecil B. and William C. De Mille, " Salvation Nell," by Edward Sheldon, " The Servant in the House," by Charles Rann Kennedy, " The Third Degree," by Charles Klein, " Vera, the Medium," by Richard Harding Davis, " Wildfire," by George V. Hobart, and " The Wolf," by Eugene Walter.

Compare that list, its virtues and lacks, with this list, *its* virtues and lacks, of the last theatrical year: " Men in White," by Sidney Kingsley, " Ah, Wilderness! ", by Eugene O'Neill, "The Green Bay Tree," by Mordaunt Shairp, "Her Master's Voice," by Clare Kummer, "Is Life Worth Living?", by Lennox Robinson, "She Loves Me Not," dramatized from the Edward Hope novel by Howard Lindsay, "Mary of Scotland," by Maxwell Anderson, "Tobacco Road," dramatized from the Caldwell novel by Jack Kirkland, "Days Without End," by Eugene O'Neill, "Oliver Oliver," by Paul Osborn, "No More Ladies," by A. E. Thomas, "Dodsworth," dramatized from the Sinclair Lewis novel by Sidney Howard, "The Wind and the Rain," by Merton Hodge, "After Such Pleasures," by Dorothy Parker, "They Shall Not Die," by John Wexley, "Moor Born," by Dan Totheroh, "Stevedore," by Paul Peters and George Sklar, "Jig Saw," by Dawn Powell, "Sailor, Beware!", by Kenyon Nicholson and Charles Robinson, "The Pursuit of Happiness," by the Langners, "The Lake," by Dorothy Massingham, "Wednesday's Child," by Leopold Atlas, "The Shining Hour," by Keith Winter, "Richard of Bordeaux," by Gordon Daviot, and "Yellow Jack," by Sidney Howard and Paul De Kruif.

Then cast your vote.

And, while you are doing some casting, cast nine-tenths of the good-old-days books right out of the window.

CHAPTER IV

The Theatre Abroad

ഗ ഗ

The day when an American dramatic critic felt it incumbent upon him to make annual summer pilgrimages to Europe in order to develop himself and his customers in lush beauties of foreign stage art is, at least for the time being, past. Not only is he perfectly safe in remaining quietly at home in the comfortable knowledge that it will be only a short time before anything worth-while over there will come sailing to him, but he is, in addition, aware from long travelled experience that he can foretell and accurately describe nine-tenths of the plays on regular European view without stirring an inch from his New York work-table. And what is more, even the remaining tenth often doesn't give him any particular descriptive trouble.

During the last summer, for example, there were in England and on the Continent probably not more than four or five plays at the outside that might have provided the critic with even fair material to write home about. The German stage, as is sufficiently known, has been completely sterilized by the Hitler government; nothing produced there since the swastika superseded the democratic dill pickle has been worth critical notice. The new plays, written largely by Hitlerian press-agents, have been in the main either cut and dried valentines of love for Adolph or dramatized college yells whooping it up for the Nazi team. All the better producers have been banished to southern Austria, where the unhappy fellows have to eke out a meagre existence in million dollar palaces, with nothing to subsist on but eight or ten meals a day, or to Switzerland, where they may loll all day in the cool, sunny breezes and spend the evenings either over a drinkable wine that costs less than sixty-five cents a bottle or at Jimmy Durante movies, or to Hollywood, where they must starve to death on a mere pittance of five thousand dollars a week.

The Russian stage, from all accounts, while it has now abandoned Soviet propaganda as its sole artistic aim, has not yet got anything like a foothold in the new ground, and is still in the embarrassing position of balancing itself delicately on the middle of a see-saw. A farce or two has attracted a bit of attention, but surely a farce or two is nothing to persuade a critic to travel four or five thousand miles, particularly if he doesn't relish a diet of black bread and dried fish and likes at least one sheet on his bed. Italy, so far as the critic has been able to determine, has turned up only an indifferent script by Pirandello and even that small prospect was suppressed by the Mussolini agents before the critic could have got downtown to buy a steamer ticket. So far, therefore, there was in the three countries named nothing to coax him, in the line of duty, away from home.

What else? In France, the theatre has been even deader than it was the year before or the year before that. And if you knew your French theatre in those years you do not have to be told how dead that is. The only two plays on exhibition in Paris during the late season that might have been of any conceivable interest were Verneuil's "Le Mari que J'ai Voulu" and Bourdet's "Les Temps Difficiles," and neither was anything calling for immediate feverish cable dispatches. The former was the more or less conventional Gallic comedy of the young girl married to a sedate oldster and of her affairs with the Clark Gables of the environs. It contained one amusing episode that brought down the first-act curtain, and also several bright little passages of dialogue, but otherwise was hardly on the stimulating side. The Bourdet play was a deliberately contrived audience-shocker that smelled of Henri Bernstein at his bernsteinest. Its theme was the sacrifice of a girl on the altar of money and her forced marriage to the idiot son of wealthy neighbors. And its much-advertised big scene consisted in the idiot's demoniacal pounding on his alarmed young wife's bedroom door in his frenzied attempt to gain access to her person. It should, I think you will agree, hardly be demanded of an American critic, however conscientious and fond of light wines and dancing, that he spend two weeks at sea in order to inform you at sober length of such a twain of art works.

We come to England. What was the top of the season's menu there? The top, that is, in the period that might have been reviewed by the critic compelled perforce to remain on the home grounds until the conclusion of the local season. A glance down the list of entries disclosed only the following as being worthy of his notice — and not any too intensive notice at that: "Escape Me Never!", by Margaret Kennedy, solely because of Elisabeth Bergner's appearance in it (and the critic had already reviewed and written of Miss Bergner's fine art for fully a dozen years, after visits to her native Germany); "Laburnum Grove," by J. B. Priestley, whose "Dangerous Corner" if not his "The Good Companions" was critically piquant; and Gordon Daviot's "Queen of Scots." Of the other possible interests, Bridie's "A Sleeping Clergyman," which the Theatre Guild has presented here this season, he would have found no longer on the boards. As for the rest, the critic would hardly feel it necessary to go to England to refamiliarize himself with "Reunion in Vienna" and the Lunts, "Biography" and Ina Claire, "The Pursuit of Happiness," "Men in White," "Counsellor-At-Law," "The Late Christopher Bean," and various other plays and performers whose aspects he had already commented on this side of Ambrose channel.

Surely there was very little, therefore, that would have called upon a steamer trunk. Germany was flat on its dramatic back; Italy produced nothing; France rested content with a couple of box-office exhibits; Hungary, erstwhile bazaar of amusing comedies, was temporarily comatose; and England, with minor exception, offered only one or two things deserving of even a modest sheet of foolscap — and then chiefly because of the actresses visible in them.

As I have observed, the critic could describe the general dramatic nine-tenths without going anywhere near them. These other nine-tenths seldom vary; year in and year out they are the same. Any American critic who has covered the European theatre for any length of time knows full well their nature before he starts packing his bags. He knows that the French stage is each season certain to disclose at least three or four farces in which various Fifis figure adulterously with various Gastons in invariant beds, the while the various Fifis' various maids carry on with the various Gastons' various valets and the various Fifis' various elderly spouses are eventually placated with the assurance that everything has been morally jake and that their deplorable suspicions have been born of evil dreams resulting from late langouste suppers with gay Folies Bergère dancers at the Boeuf Sur Le Toit. He knows, too, that the same stage every season is sure to reveal at least three or four polite comedies in which the same Fifis, Gastons, maids and valets do the selfsame thing somewhat more *largo* and *piano* and in which the elderly husbands (usually depicted as senile at the advanced age

of forty) pretend in the last act that they have seen nothing, kiss their wives a fond and tender good-night and,
when the latter are safely in bed, move cautiously to the
telephone, lower their voices to a whisper, and make dates
with gay dancers from the Casino de Paris. And he knows,
also, that at the same time there will be running two or
three very grave and serious dramas in which exactly the
same stuff, minus only the maids and valets, will be treated
largo di molto, with an occasional sudden *fortississimo*
passage that has all the volume of a Black Tom explosion,
and in which the final curtain will descend upon the spectacle of the elderly husbands either forgiving their young
wives their trespasses and folding them again nobly to
their bosoms, amid much contrite sniffling on the part of
both parties to the embrace, or upon the spectacle of the
old boys magnanimously turning their young wives over
to the younger Gastons with sad shakes of the head and
even sadder philosophical animadversions upon the even
still sadder fact that age must ever be defeated by youth
in the lists of love.

Nor does the English stage, in *its* other nine-tenths,
offer the American critic of any experience much greater
prognosticating difficulty. He knows that he is bound to
descry at least two or three productions of Shakespearean
plays sponsored by former and somewhat antiquated London dramatic critics who believe that the defects of the productions in the way of acting can be concealed by the
simple expedient of staging them out of doors, where the

audiences, if any, will be distracted by the loud twittering
of birds and the bites of insects. He knows, also, that he
will find at least three comedies, generally adaptations
from the French or Spanish, in which English actor-
managers past their sixty-fifth birthday will present themselves as pertinacious old beaux who embarrass and
confound their sons and nephews with their excessive spry-
ness and virtuosity in the arts of amour; at least two farces
which, upon their importation to New York, will be
hauled off to the storehouse after less than a week's run
and which nevertheless, for no decipherable reason, will
keep on playing in London for two whole seasons; one or
two plays dealing with British school-boy life or with the
life of the teachers, in which the leading woman will have
a wistful affair with the youthful hero, who wistfully
won't know what it is all about; and three plays written
by elderly spinsters in which the heroine, an elderly spinster, enjoys a rapturous hour of love with the handsome
young hero (his name in all likelihood Robin) either on
a Tyrolean hillside, or in a Scotch stone quarry, or some
other such fanciedly romantic if damned uncomfortable
spot. Then, in addition, there are sure to be several imitations of Chekhov by London playwrights just graduated
from their 'teens, in which the repressed young wife of
the master of the house, a bastard if ever there was one,
will at the conclusion of the second act throw herself passionately into the arms of any male character who can
play the piano, provided only he was gassed in the war;

[63]

Ruth Draper; a couple of revivals of the less interesting plays of Galsworthy and Granville-Barker; two plays dealing with the life of either an actress or a ballet dancer which will give the leading woman an opportunity to run the gamut of age from nineteen to ninety and which will display her at the end, despite her valetudinarian makeup, as full of the old pep as Mae West; an assortment of mystery and detective plays that differ from their American kind only in the somewhat more precise English speech of the dicks; and at least one play in which some hero of American history like Lincoln, Robert E. Lee or John Brown will, in the British handling, be quite indistinguishable from Sir Thomas Beecham or Mr. Cyril Maude.

With Germany out of the dramatic running at the present time, with Italy in the dramatic doldrums, and with Russia, as noted, not yet clearly emancipated, what is there then left for the American critic to hornswoggle his susceptible readers with? Unless he has the critical Barnum instinct, nothing. If he is gifted with the aforementioned instinct, however, he can always pretend to discover something pretty rich and juicy. He can take a trip to Finland, for instance, and profess to find there such a repertoire company as has never been seen in the world before, and he can probably get away with it because nobody ever goes to Finland. Denmark, a bit closer to the lane of travel, he has to be a little more cautious about, though he can take a chance on some theoretically admirable dance troupe there, as Americans abroad seldom go in for such things and wouldn't know the difference between what was good and bad even if they did. Stockholm, too, is generally pretty safe, as a translated Eugene O'Neill play is usually on tap and as the critic can always write an article elaborately specifying how very much better acted it was in Sweden than in New York. And, of course, there is always Salzburg, at least for readers who have never been there and take a strange delight in reading annually the same account of the open air performance of " Jedermann."

But the punctilious critic gags at such obvious shenanigan. As things stand in Europe today, he feels that he can better serve the critical art and the art of drama by staying at home and devoting himself to Mr. Billy Rose's Music Hall.

CHAPTER V

Critical Presumptions — Theatrical

No. 1 is the critical legend that everything that Mr. George S. Kaufman writes or touches promptly turns into box-office gold. That Mr. Kaufman is one of the real talents of our American theatre, no one, I hope, will deny; but that, like us lesser talents, he has never known failure is believed only by those commentators who keep their records on their cuffs and who are given to the fashionable habit of changing their shirts once a week. Mr. Kaufman has had his numerous successes, but he has also, alas, had his various blue moments. "Here Today," which he carpentered, staged and personally invested in, was anything but prosperous. "The Dark Tower," upon which he collaborated and in the production of which he assisted, got a very short distance either in New York, or, subsequently, in London. "Let 'Em Eat Cake," another collaboration, was far from being a shining gold tooth, and "Eldorado," another man's manuscript on which he volunteered to work for a while, never got beyond the rewriting. "Someone in the House" and "Jacques Duval," his earliest efforts, were only too quickly forgotten, even, and graciously, by himself. The musical show " Helen of Troy " and the collaborative " Deep Tangled Wildwood," ditto. Neither " Minick " nor " The Good Fellow," also collaborations, proved any too profitable. And " The Channel Road," still another collaboration, was a box-office dud. . . . No criticism of the merit or lack thereof in these plays and shows is intended; our interest is simply in what is legend and what is fact.

No. 2 is the so-called *Wunderkind,* in other words, Mr. Jed Harris. As in the case of Mr. Kaufman, it is a more or less popular critical superstition that the acumen of Mr. Harris is so rich and rare that all he has to do to rule the roost is to take almost any kind of manuscript, promptly get the author to re-write it (or do the job himself), and then put it on a stage under his own directorial supervision. Also as in the case of Mr. Kaufman, there is no denying the fact that this Mr. Harris is an exceptionally shrewd and very skilful theatrical personage; but, once again, facts are facts. Cast your eye over the *Wunderkind's* lesser record and look upon the other side of his successful picture. " The Wiser They Are " got absolutely nowhere, nor did " The Fatal Alibi." Mr. Gilhooley " was a failure, and " The Lake " was a sorry botch. " Wonder Boy " fell far short of success, as did the production of " The Inspector General." " Serena Blandish " was a box-office disappointment and " Spread Eagle " followed suit. As for some of Mr. Harris' greatest successes, they were staged not by himself, if we are to believe the playbills, but by other hands. "The Royal Family" bore the staging name of Mr. David Burton; "Front Page" gave credit for direction to Mr. George S. Kaufman; "Coquette" gave credit to Mr. George Abbott; and "Broadway" gave credit to the same Mr. Abbott, plus Philip Dunning. As with all of us mortals, there would also seem to be two sides to the eminent Mr. Harris' handsome oil painting.

But a temporary halt to such "success stories" and a veering to somewhat more lofty considerations. So to No. 3. This is the critical insistence upon Miss Katharine Cornell as "the first lady of the theatre." That Miss Cornell is a lady, I am only too willing to proclaim, if necessary, from the housetops, but that Miss Cornell is, in sociopolitical terminology, the *first* one of the theatre I fear I must gainsay. Is it possible that our young critical eulogists of Miss Cornell have forgotten Miss Margaret Anglin, an actress whose accomplishments over a very long span of years reduce those of Miss Cornell, in comparison, to what remains still almost an amateur level? To anyone who knows our theatre in its last thirty and more years, Miss Anglin's record, which ranges all the histrionic way from Sophocles to Shakespeare and from "Monte Cristo" through Bronson Howard to "The Great Divide" and which embraces a career as leading woman to celebrated actors all the way from James O'Neill and Richard Mansfield to E. H. Sothern and Henry Miller, must seem to take at least a measure of precedence over the considerably younger Miss Cornell's. While the latter's is a nice enough record in its small way, one can yet hardly see wherein has lain the particularly super-eminent *kudos* of performances in things like " The Green Hat," " Nice People," " Dishonored Lady " and other such Broadway one-finger exercises. This season we shall have got a line on Miss Cornell's true talents when she appears as Shakespeare's Juliet. But up until now, for her claim to the title of first lady of our theatre, she has offered us, aside from such histrionic one-finger exercises, only a serviceable and attractive ingénue performance in " A Bill of Divorcement "; admittedly deficient performances of the name rôles in both Clemence Dane's " Will Shakespeare " and André Obey's " Lucrèce "; pleasant enough but wholly unimportant performances of unimportant rôles in such unimportant plays as " The Enchanted Cottage " (that dish of mush by Pinero out of Barrie), " The Outsider " (that geyser of hokum), " Casanova " (that couturière's parade), " The Way Things Happen " (that Owen Davis exhibit written by an Englishwoman), " The Age of Innocence " (that box-office pat on grandma's back) and " Alien Corn " (that that); a routine, old-time melodrama performance in " The Letter "; an intelligent and quite lovely performance in " Candida "; and an even more intelligent and lovelier performance in " The Barretts of Wimpole Street." If, on that record, Miss Cornell is the First Lady of the theatre, all I can say is that, on hers, Miss Anglin must be the President.

No. 4, a critical conviction of more recent birth, is the apparently unanimous belief that, because in " Days Without End " he wrote a pro-Catholic play, Eugene O'Neill, himself born a Catholic, has therefore, after years of wobbling, unquestionably now gone back to Holy Church hook, line and sinker. If Mr. O'Neill has been inside a Catholic or any other kind of church in the last thirty years, or thirty days, save perhaps on the occasion of a close relative's funeral, no one in his confidence has been apprised of it — but that is not the point. The point is rather the common critical presumption that the moment a writer writes eloquently about anything, he must necessarily believe in it heart and soul. This, of course, is pure nonsense. It is possible that Mr. O'Neill may in the future come to spend twenty-four hours of every day in the year in a Catholic church, but simply because he wrote " Days Without End " no more soundly predicts any such commendable act than " The Hairy Ape " predicts his fistic espousal of Communism, " Dynamo " his intention of going to his Maker in the turbine room of the Westinghouse Electrical Company, or " Diff'rent " his immediate decision to hang himself.

No. 5 will doubtless bring with it the general blind, ecstatic critical endorsement, upon its return engagement here this season, of the same Abbey Theatre troupe that sent the reviewers' hats kiting high in the air last season. That this troupe, whatever its virtues, no more represents the Abbey Theatre at its acting best than the current Berlin ex-Reinhardt theatre companies represent the former theatres at theirs, is news one feels one must immodestly impart to the deluded reviewers. This company, in the histrionic chronological line, is the third of the Abbey acting groups. The first, a really remarkable organization, contained, it will be recalled, such excellent artists as Arthur Sinclair, Fred O'Donovan, Dudley Digges, the inimitable elder Fay, Sara Allgood, Marie O'Neill, *et al.* The second, for all the withdrawal of Digges, Fay, and a few minor others, was still made up of most of the original members. Then came, along with Sean O'Casey's disgusted severance of his relations with the Abbey, the complete disruption. Digges came to America; Sinclair, O'Donovan and the Misses Allgood and O'Neill decided to go it on their own in England; and others, too, went their independent ways. And what was left, to put it in the most liberal and politest of terms, was merely a gathering together, almost indiscriminately, of a third-hand troupe of assiduous understudies and feeble echoes. This is the troupe that comes to us under the proud original Abbey Theatre label. This is the troupe that the reviewers confuse with the splendid acting tradition of the Abbey Theatre. This is the troupe that gets their befuddled hallelujahs.

No. 6 is the venerable critical ventilation as to the invariable superiority of the writing in the majority of English plays to that in the majority of American. It is entirely true that there was a day, and not so long ago, when the writing in the average English product was very considerably superior to that in its local equivalent, but that day is past. (Let it be remembered that we are speaking of the *average* play.) At the present time, England coughs up just as large a proportion of bad stage writing as we do. And often an even larger. Make a few comparisons, for example, from last season's record. Was the writing in Ivor Novello's " Party " any better, or even so good, as that in, say, that no more meritorious exhibit, " The Blue Widow "? Was the writing revealed in " Ten Minute Alibi " any better, or even so good, as that in the American-made mystery dingus called " Invitation to a Murder "? Compare the writing in " Eight Bells " to that in the American drip called " Heat Lightning," in " Strange Orchestra " to that in " The Perfumed Lady," in " Come of Age " to that in " Oliver Oliver," in " Come What May " to " Jig Saw," in " These Two " even to " The Wooden Slipper." Was " John Brown's " writing in any way superior to that in any dozen average local products, deserved failures as well? I leave it to the jury.

No. 7 continues to contact us, as the high-toned trade phrase is, with the questionable critical habit of declaring a foreign actress a great genius on the score of a single reviewed performance. Miss Elisabeth Bergner, who has played here this season for the first time, is an actress in point and the fact that she is, in truth, one of very uncommon talent does not make the aforesaid habit any the less questionable. This habit, as native to England as to

America — the English critics hailed Miss Bergner as one of the greatest living actresses after seeing her in but one play — reduces criticism to a level of journalistic sensationalism. In the case of an actress of restricted range as, for example, Yvonne Printemps, a more or less complete appraisal may be made on the cue of a single performance, since the talents of the actress in point are uniformly suited to and employed in a single species of drama. But to pretend fully to estimate a so variedly versatile actress as Miss Bergner, who is as apt at Shakespeare as at minor modern comedy, after observing her in a single play by Margaret Kennedy is to be, however accidentally the bull's-eye may be hit, critically suspect and a little ridiculous. Miss Bergner, as anyone who has seen her many and various performances in Germany sufficiently knows, is a fine and flexible artist, but one may be pardoned for being skeptical of the kind of criticism which proclaims her as such simply because it finds her very good in a single small comedy. It is much as if Miss Jane Cowl played her admirable Juliet in Germany and, because of that one excellent performance, was hailed by German critics as the greatest of American actresses.

CHAPTER VI

Critical Presumptions — General

༷ ༷

Ambrose Bierce. — Whenever I meet a man with a pretense to critical sagacity in the matter of American *belles lettres,* I have an annoying habit of asking him his opinion of the late lost, strayed or stolen Mr. Ambrose Bierce. If, upon the question, he imparts to me a crisp wink, I put him down in my mental files as a fellow worth cultivating. If, on the other hand, he goes into an encomiastic clog, I dismiss him as one whose critical faculties have still not outgrown their adolescence. For I believe that an admiration of Bierce, among men of my generation, is invariably an unconscious hangover from the enthusiasm of their youth, when an epigram — provided only it were sufficiently cynical — was the last word in worldly wisdom and when any story of the occult in which the tall grass was mysteriously agitated by something (spelled with a capital S) was a dark-shudderful masterpiece.

Bierce's persistent reputation as an eminento of letters is undoubtedly due to these long-pants laudators with an unrevoked short-pants rapture. Certainly a sedulous scrutiny of his collected works reveals little adult basis for it. He was, at his best, little more — in " The Monk and the Hangman's Daughter " (a paraphrase of a translation by Danziger of Richard Voss) — than a prelusive George Sylvester Viereck; little more — in " Can Such Things Be? " and " Tales of Soldiers and Civilians " (" In the Midst of Life ") — than a somewhat superior *Black Cat* magazine writer. His fables in " Cobwebs From an Empty Skull " and in " Fantastic Fables " are second-rate Alfred Polgar and fifth-rate Dunsany. And as for his " Write It Right," the title itself provides abundantly illuminating criticism. As editor of *The Argonaut* and *The Wasp,* Bierce had his points, but his so-called Prattle columns, which he contributed for years to the San Francisco *Examiner,* when re-read today seem pitiably weak and empty beside the columns of such men as Heywood Broun, Westbrook Pegler, *et al*.

It is the consistent custom of Bierce's champions, however, to meet any such derogatory appraisal of his literary performances with the proud exclamation, " Ah, but what of ' The Devil's Dictionary '! " This " Devil's Dictionary " is not only one of their powerful legends, but one of literary America's at large. It is held out as the paragon of true and devastating wit, the trump of polished, crystallized acid. Well, take a look at it. I open it and quote a few samples from under the A's alone; they sufficiently suggest the flavor of what is under the B's, C's, D's and on to the Z's:

Abasement, *n.* A decent and customary mental attitude in the presence of wealth or power. Peculiarly appropriate in an employee when addressing an employer.

Abdication, *n.* An act whereby a sovereign attests his sense of the high temperature of the throne.

Abscond, *v.i.* To "move in a mysterious way," commonly with the property of another.

Academe, *n.* An ancient school where morality and philosophy were taught. Academy, *n.* (from academe). A modern school where football is taught.

Admiral, *n.* That part of a war-ship which does the talking while the figure-head does the thinking.

Admonition, *n.* Gentle reproof, as with a meat-axe.

Affianced, *pp.* Fitted with an ankle-ring for the ball-and-chain.

Ambidextrous, *adj.* Able to pick with equal skill a right-hand pocket or a left.

Anoint, *v.t.* To grease a king or other great functionary already sufficiently slippery.

Apothecary, *n.* The physician's accomplice, undertaker's benefactor and grave worm's provider.

Appeal, *v.t.* In law, to put the dice into the box for another throw.

April Fool, *n.* The March fool with another month added to his folly.

Architect, *n.* One who drafts a plan of your house, and plans a draft of your money.

Armor, *n.* The kind of clothing worn by a man whose tailor is a blacksmith.

Arsenic, *n*. A kind of cosmetic greatly affected by the ladies, whom it greatly affects in turn.

Gentlemen, I ask you!

One speculates as to the origins of the notion that Bierce was a considerable somebody. Like the late Richard Harding Davis, he had a superficially impressive front and a superficially impressive manner; these, as they often do, may have contrived to make certain impressionable men confound the big brass sign outside the bank for the amount of gold in its vault. He had, in addition, a romantic Civil War record, and a romantic war record isn't a bad asset to any writer, particularly in the minds of his contemporary critics who have served in the commissary department, or as pot-bearers in field hospitals and butlers to the General's horse. And there were a number of such in the Civil War. Further, in the San Francisco of his day, Bierce — with his large manner and small competence — was a big toad in a little hole. He looked important; he comported himself importantly; he spouted importantly. He possessed the faculty of investing himself with a certain degree of awesomeness, like a movie actor in the city to the south today who has a Picasso in his bathroom and has once had a Duke stay over-night in his house. What was more, he had that most precious of all speciously impressive gifts: the air of a man who always seemed superior and independent and, even when without a sou in the world, at perfect and lofty ease among those with ample funds.

[77]

In every smaller city, there is and always has been some writer or newspaper man who is singled out for matinée-idolizing by his cronies and certain of the town folk. It is a matter partly of local pride and partly of the average man's insistent need to number among his friends and acquaintances someone, however essentially dubious, to talk about, brag about, and in a degree look up to. In every newspaper office in every such city there is one such great hero. Bierce was the selection in the San Francisco of his time. And it was not long thereafter that he was advertised broadcast by his loving friends in the same ecstatic breath with the California climate, the size of the redwood trees, the sunset on the Golden Gate, and the one-dollar girls in Chinatown.

The first and biggest fall-guy was that charming fellow, the late Percival Pollard. Percy — God rest his good soul — was the greatest discoverer of his critical period. Hardly a week passed that he didn't discover a tremendous genius in one corner of the globe or another. In his day, Percy discovered geniuses by the wholesale and by the freight carload. The only trouble with the great majority of his geniuses was that they didn't seem to have much noticeable talent. But that never deterred Percy, as a glance through his critical manifestoes will attest. Percy's geniuses ranged all the way from *Schuhplättler* in Munich cabarets to female Polish mystics and from mural-painter graduates of comic weeklies to the more comely French young girl aphrodisiacal poets. And in due time and in the natural course of events, Bierce took his place in the Pollard Hall of Fame. That was the send-off, and it was not very long afterward that the younger critics, offshoots of the old *Criterion* school of which Percy was a constituent, began on their own imitatively to discover Bierce all over again. It is these younger critics, now grown to more or less venerable manhood, who — along with their still small and enthusiastic Bierce-reading sons — continue to foster the Bierce legend.

სა სა

David Graham Phillips. — I have made bold to ascribe the legend of the genius of Ambrose Bierce to the persistent sentimentality (and ignorance) of present-day adults still in their 1890-5 literary diapers. It is my point that it is these uncritical and unwitting throwbacks to youngsterdom who, not taking the trouble to reappraise the enthusiasms of their youth, are largely responsible for perpetuating the doctrine that Bierce, a third-rater if ever there lived one, was a piercing wit, a devastating iconoclastic mind, and a very high-toned literary artist. In the same way I should like to call attention to another great literary hero of the critics and public of twenty-five years ago, and make equally bold to analyze him in the light of a current rereading.

This second hero is David Graham Phillips who, during his lifetime and for some years thereafter, was widely hailed as one of the greatest of American realists and as one of the finest of American novelists. In this last year I have undertaken, in the services of truth and the national honor, to read again every book that he wrote, and I emerge from the grand plunge with the conviction that, if here was an important realistic mind and an important novelist, I am either the poorest judge of intellectual and literary values this side of Columbia University or one whom the wholesale reading in question has paralyzed out of all possibly nascent critical talent.

Although Phillips impressed the infrallectuals of his time as a gratifyingly well-barbered and well-tailored Dreiser, he was essentially little more than a Robert W. Chambers out of an Upton Sinclair. In even the best of his realistic writing a kind of pretty-pretty quality refractorily permeated the scene. And always one had the feeling — as one still has on re-reading him — that his realism was the residuum of suckled indignation rather than of actual experience. He was, as the more modern psychologists would quickly have observed, a snob who envied and even loved the things he professed to hate. He could write, but the blood in his eye blinded him to himself. He was, subconsciously, the squire of his worst villains.

These villains were (*1*) women, (*2*) money, and (*3*) the world of fashionable society. In one way or another, the bulk of his writing concerned one or the other or all of them. His three earliest works, " The Great God Success," " Her Serene Highness " and " A Woman Ventures," consisted in a savage attack upon the American *haut monde* and the women who were part of it. " The Master Rogue " was a savage attack upon millionaires, as " The Social Secretary " was an attemptedly sardonic one. " Light-Fingered Gentry " again attacked the plutocratic *haut monde.* " Old Wives For New," his best work, paid its author's usual compliments to the millionaire, and to woman. " The Fashionable Adventures of Joshua Craig " again touched upon money and ladies of high social standing, as " The Hungry Heart " had to do with a Southern mazuma magnifico and his disconsolate spouse. " The Husband's Story " hammered yet again at the rich American snob, chiefly female. And, " Susan Lenox: Her Fall and Rise," written for one of the Hearst magazines, underneath its tin-pot movie melodrama plied the same old artillery against social and economic snobberies.

Whatever the variance of approach, the animus at the bottom of almost all these novels was generally the same: the animus of a somewhat bedraggled bird longing for a golden cage that was not open to it. Even when allowing, in a magnanimous gesture of fairness, glints of virtue to such rich and lofty personages as otherwise he literarily goosed, Phillips could barely conceal his disrelish in betraying even for a moment his own ingrained admiration of them. He performed constantly a vasectomy on his own secret personal ambitions, and the resulting pain became his sterile literary diatribes. That he could write, it must be repeated; but to strike a balance between what he passionately believed and what he passionately tried personally for his own obsequious comfort to forget, was within neither his power nor his talent. The self-depuratory faculty that is the gift of the true artist was denied him.

Phillips was, above all else, first and foremost simply an indignant melodramatist. In his attempted excursions into humor, traces of the indignant melodramatist still stubbornly revealed themselves. He was a blood-and-thunder show at five dollars a seat, doubling psychologically as the hero and villain, and sometimes even as Little Nell. It was natural, therefore, that in the turmoil his crusader self often confusedly presented itself in fierce black moustachios, the while his darker rôle surprised everyone with a beautiful curly blond wig. He was a realist self-manufactured in a stage dressing-room. The moment he emerged into the light of day, his make-up was disconcertingly evident.

The National Mockery. — The first of the great popular American critical jokes is the governmental Vice-President. The mere mention of the Vice-President, whoever he may be, is good for a laugh any time. The comic papers thrive on it; the humor of one of the biggest stage successes of recent seasons, " Of Thee I Sing," is based almost entirely upon it; the columnists rely upon it at least twice a week to produce a chuckle; the caricaturists and car-

[82]

toonists would not know what to do if the Government were to eliminate the office; and the movie comedians duly get into line with their sure-fire facetiæ. But just where and how the idea that the Vice-President is a subject for unrestrained mirth originally got under way is rather hard to make out. For a study of the Vice-Presidential statistics hardly uncovers any considerable grounds for low comedy. On the contrary, it reveals the fact that what the American public makes a joke of is really anything but a custard pie matter.

Consider. In the popular humor, the Vice-President is visualized as a completely negligible figure, a fifth wheel on even a wheelbarrow, yet five of the gentry have found themselves suddenly lodged in the Presidential chair upon the death or assassination of the Chief Executive: John Tyler upon the death of William Henry Harrison after only a month in office; Millard Fillmore upon the death of Zachary Taylor; Andrew Johnson upon the assassination of Lincoln; Chester A. Arthur upon the assassination of Garfield; and Theodore Roosevelt upon the assassination of McKinley. Only a shot that went wild, fired by a house-painter at President Jackson, kept another Vice-President from sudden occupation of the Presidential throne. And still another Vice-President almost overnight might have found himself the Chief Executive of the Republic had Woodrow Wilson's sudden partial paralysis by apoplexy on a Western campaign trip been a trifle more serious.

[83]

Let us scrutinize the materials of the Vice-President joke a little further. Aaron Burr was a Vice-President, and what if accident had lodged him in the Presidential chair? What humor there? John Adams, Thomas Jefferson, Martin Van Buren and Calvin Coolidge were Vice-Presidents who subsequently became Presidents. If, therefore, the Vice-President is a joke, in many cases why is not the President also, in the popular critical imagination, quite as much of a joke? Why the illogical discrimination? And what, incidentally, was so very funny about Vice-Presidents like Elbridge Gerry, John C. Calhoun, John C. Breckinridge, Schuyler Colfax, Levi P. Morton, or even Daniel D. Tompkins, Adlai E. Stevenson and James S. Sherman?

The second of the great American popular jokes is the laziness of the Southern Negro. In the general national conception, the darky below the Mason-Dixon line is perfectly willing to call it a day after he has snoozed for six hours in the warm sun, eaten three watermelons, shot two games of craps, and played one tune on his banjo. That he does any genuine work is seldom believed. Yet, according to the latest available statistics, there are 95,203 active Negro farmers in Alabama, or one for every one and one-half native white; 72,282 in Arkansas, or one for every one and one-half native white; almost 130,000 in Florida, or one for every three native white; more than 130,000 in Georgia, where there are only 180,000 native white; 62,-000 in Louisiana as against 71,000 native white; 161,219 in Mississippi and only 110,279 native white (it was in Mississippi, incidentally, that the joke about the indolent darky started); more than 76,000 in North Carolina, or one for every one and five-eighths native white; 109,000 in South Carolina, where the native white farmers number only a little over 83,000; almost 79,000 in Texas, and 48,-000 in Virginia.

The third of the nation's popular critical jests is that nobody in New York has any money but the Jews, the Jews have garnered all of it. In the last official tentative valuation of personal property of New Yorkers, forty-three persons were listed as being in what is roughly known as the millionaire class. In the list there were just three Jews. In the same official valuation of wealthy estates thirty-six persons were listed. In the list were just seven Jews. In the same official valuation of personal fortunes somewhat less than a million, but in the higher ranges of the hundreds of thousands, 110 persons were named. In the list were eighteen Jews.

The fourth of the American's favorite laughs is a series of American towns that includes Peoria, Kalamazoo, Ypsilanti, Hoboken, Oshkosh, Yonkers, Keokuk, Walla Walla, Punxsutawney, Kankakee, Kokomo, Cheboygan and Dubuque (whose residents are made up entirely of old ladies). The precise reason for the popular jocosity is not readily determinable. If it is based on the humorous sound of the names of the towns, why isn't Opelika every bit as funny as Peoria, Tuscaloosa every bit as comical as Kala-

[85]

mazoo, McGehee good for a laugh as loud as Ypsilanti, and Azusa, Sausalito, Watseka, Mishawaka, Oskaloosa, Osawatomie, Bogalusa or Natchitoches as funny as any of the others named? Why do not Americans, if they respond to comical sounds, favor with their guffaws — instead of Hoboken, Yonkers and Dubuque, which really aren't so funny — such towns as Opelousas, Ipswich, Seekonk, Hamtramck, Inskster, Ishepeming, Owosso, Yazoo City, Secaucus, Pawhuska, Wewoka, Emaus, Lititz, Mauch Chunk, Moosic, Perkasie, Waxahachie, Wink, Yoakum, Winooski, Puyallup, Kaukauna and Oconomowoc, all figuring on the same map?

If it is not the names of the towns but the towns themselves that set the popular laugh in motion, can it be that the towns are absurd failures and have so become the targets of ridicule? Investigating this side of the question, we find that the popular laughter has not only not hurt the towns in point, but has actually helped them. Instead of dissuading people from them, it has apparently brought people to them. The last census shows that, in the very decade when jokes about the towns were thickest, Peoria's population jumped from 76,000 to 105,000, Kalamazoo's increased more than 6,000, Ypsilanti's gain was almost a third over its entire previous population, and that every other one of the towns, with the single exception of Hoboken, disclosed like healthy increases. In the case of Hoboken, it may parenthetically be noted that the falling off of jokes at its expense doubtless paradoxically may have had something to do with its population decline. Either that or the quality of New Jersey beer.

The fifth of the American critical humors is that section of the country called the Bible Belt. In other words, the strip running through Tennessee and embracing the contiguous states. The real Bible Belt, however, the statistics reveal, is not this strip of the nation at all, but the strip running through unholy eastern Pennsylvania through sinful New York and New Jersey. Five hundred and seventy-three to one is the exact ratio of Bibles sold annually in this latter strip as against the number sold in the former.

Popular mockery No. 6 is the speedy evanescence of Hollywood marriages which, according to the popular jocular idea, are ready to celebrate their diamond jubilees if they last a week. Yet a study of the New York " Social Register," together with the divorce and re-marriage statistics related to its personages, indicates that Hollywood is a rather old-fashioned marriage community compared with the metropolitan social colony.

We come to the seventh and final item in the great American critical cachinnation, to wit, the dunderheadedness of the college boy. This is one of the cardinal articles in the catalogue of American humor. According to the aforesaid article, the boy who goes to college spends all of his time in a raccoon coat, however warm the weather, and, when he isn't drinking gin out of a pocket flask and shouting rah-rah, is either holding hands with imbecile flappers or drinking more gin out of a pocket flask and shouting rah-rah. He learns nothing, wastes his father's good money and would be much better off, so far as his future goes, if he didn't go to college and began work in an office at eighteen. The boy who sells papers until he is ten and then goes to work in an office, on the other hand, is the one destined to do great things in the world.

A glance at the statistics published in the latest edition of "Who's Who in America," as well as those published in the preceding editions, hardly supports the American laugh at the college loafer's expense. "Who's Who in America," as is sufficiently known, lists all those Americans who have achieved signal success and eminence in their chosen fields of enterprise. Well, what do we find? We find, according to the latest figures, that eighty-five out of each one hundred persons furnishing educational data attended college and that seventy-three of each one hundred were graduated.

"One of the noticeable differences in the totals appearing in the educational statistics of 'Who's Who in America' during years past," say the editors, "is the growth of the college-trained as compared with those who never attended college. The first four tabulations, ranging from 1899 to 1911, showed that of those who supplied educational data, collegians represented sixty-nine to seventy-one per cent of the names, or that about seventy out of one hundred had received college training.

"The volume for 1916–17, with a greater number of

names, disclosed an increase to 72.88 per cent, while the edition for 1922–23, with 22,075 names, gave a further increase to 77.36 per cent in ratio of collegians. The highest percentage of all is shown in the tabulation of the 28,805 names listed in the 1928–29 edition, 85.09 per cent of those reporting educational data in that edition having attended college."

The editors conclude with this observation: "This growth is doubtless due to the fact that the steadily increasing complexity of the social and economic structure of modern life demands more highly educated leaders, the standards of admission to 'Who's Who in America' having remained the same from the first."

The above figures are especially significant, the editors point out, when considered in connection with the statement in the United States census that only 4.55 per cent of the population of the United States above the age of twenty-one is college trained. This means, the editors emphasize, that at the present time 4.55 per cent of the total population of the country provides the eighty-odd per cent of the outstanding personages listed in "Who's Who in America." It means also that the remaining 95.45 per cent of the population of the country contributes only 16.95 per cent of "Who's Who" notables.

ص ص

Mens Nana In Corpore Sano. — That, taking one with another, women's minds are less clean than men's is a fact which, while sufficiently recognized by men in the mass, has yet strangely, so far as I know, not found its commentator and analyst on paper. We have had a few general epigrams on the subject, and we have thought, now and again, that we were about to read some sharp and penetrating affidavit on the matter, but in both cases delicate evasion and polite half-statement have been the only reward of our curiosity. In the interests of lovely truth, therefore, let us make bold to pursue the inquiry a bit further.

Any man who moves about in feminine society and who is not deaf in both ears can testify to the fact that women's conversation, whatever the specific nature of its initial impulse, sooner or later is inevitably bound to get around to sex. The manœuvre may be contrived indirectly and with a certain spurious show of neo-Victorian modesty — in some instances; but once it gains a measure of confidence it stalks into the topic like a bouncer into a barroom. Whereas men, when they enter into the subject, customarily enter into it, often somewhat disconcertingly, with what may metaphorically be described as both feet, women begin by skirting around its edges, by tossing out innuendo, and by playing ping-pong with suggestiveness before getting to the main business of the conversational meeting. A man will say, frankly, openly, and plainly, what is in his mind; a woman will by verbal by-play and insinuation convert what would otherwise be forthrightly clean into something that is vaguely dirty. Women seldom, in sex matters, use the straight-forward, clean-cut, appropriate terms. They rely upon circumlocutions and synonyms which, like burlesque-show strippers, are twice as suggestive as the naked words. They drape their colloquies in gauze veils and, slowly and with deliberately timed oral movements and gestures, remove them, to their twofold — or sevenfold — eroticism.

For this, the still remaining double standard of sex — it still remains for all the vociferous verbal and physical promiscuity of a relative handful of females and for all the editorial fulminations in liberal publications edited by unwanted old maids or fed-up married men who have eyes for their stenographers and obliquely wish to give their wives the gate — the still operative double standard, as I say, is doubtless responsible. Women, under its terms, are denied the privilege of directness and honesty and must perforce take refuge in an arsenal of allusive hints and winks. Their thoughts may be the same as men's thoughts, but the forbidden direct articulation of them serves by repression to make them gradually stagnant and funguscovered. A man, as the saying is, gets them off his chest and is done with them; a woman is not equally permitted to get them off her mind, and there they remain to crawl about with their increasingly slimy worminess.

This enforced repression seeking vicarious outlet is indicated, among other things, by the stuff that women read. Who are the chief consumers of cheap sex novels and magazines of so-called snappy fiction? The sales statistics show, and emphatically, that they are women —

young, medium, and pretty old. The phrase, " shop-girl fiction," tells its own story. On the higher literary but equally sexy level, who have been and are the chief wor-shippers of D. H. Lawrence, particularly in his " Lady Chatterley's Lover " mood? The answer is too obvious to be recorded.

Women think of sex in the daytime as well as at night, whereas men in general seldom find their thoughts hovering about the topic when the sun is shining. Even Frenchmen and the Viennese hardly begin before twi-light. And speculation is inflammation. I have known many men in my lifetime, but I have yet to encounter one who talked or thought about sex at lunch. The majority of women, on the other hand, even those who have to work for a living, allow their imaginations and conversa-tion to play around it from the first application of the morning lipstick to the last dab of cold cream at night. Like hatred, sex must be articulated or, like hatred, it will produce a disturbing internal malaise. The edicts of polite society are responsible to no small degree for women's dirty minds.

Any psychoanalyst or practitioner of psychopathol-ogy will tell you that, out of every ten customers and patients, nine are women. And out of the nine, at least eight will be found to be troubled with sex complexes. These sex complexes, the aforesaid professors need hardly tell you, are the result of repressions, and the aforesaid repressions are responsible for all kinds of mental quirks.

The injunction, " Get it out of your mind," suggests the nature of the mind and its thoughts. These thoughts are not healthy, but diseased. Concentration on sex, though sometimes unsuspected, has brought with it a species of mental corruption.

Plays dealing with abnormality always find their chief customers among women. When " The Captive " was, previous to its enforced withdrawal by the police, shown in New York, the box-office statistics revealed that five women to every man attended it, and the matinées were patronized almost exclusively by women.

Such pornographic literary trash as Elinor Glyn's " Three Weeks," the Mlle. Hull's " The Sheik," and Arlen's " The Green Hat " finds itself in the best-seller class solely because of women.

The sex moving pictures, with Mae West's alone excepted (and they are humorous rather than erotically stimulating), are patronized overwhelmingly, the exhibitors' records assure us, by women.

The heroines of men are Joan of Arc, Florence Nightingale and Edith Cavell. The heroines of women are Du Barry, Pompadour and Gabriele d'Annunzio.

I have lately had the privilege of scrutinizing the account books of the four leading purveyors of so-called erotica in New York City. Not the cheap dispensers of contemptible pink-backs, but the sellers of books that, for one reason or another, are not supposed to be read by the moral element in the community. The account books of the first, covering the period from January first, 1934, to July first, 1934, showed that his customers numbered 1,810 women as against 254 men. The books of the second, covering a like period, showed 927 women as against forty-six men. Those of the third, covering the time from January first, 1934, to September first, 1934, showed 737 women and only thirty-four men. And those of the fourth, covering the period from February first, 1934, to August first, 1934, disclosed 462 women as against just fourteen men. I am not acquainted with the sellers of pink-backs, and so, unfortunately, cannot offer statistics in that quarter. But the story on the somewhat higher sex level is sufficiently illuminating. Men usually outgrow their taste for pornography after they have completed, at an early age, the prescribed course of "Only a Boy," "Fanny Hill" and "Green Girls in Paris." But women's taste for pornography seems seldom to abate.

Perhaps in no clearer way may we appreciate the dubious quality of the feminine mind than by referring to the question of motion picture censorship and observing the peculiar aberrations of that mind when it serves on the various state censorship committees whose business it is to pass on the morality of the films. Through various esoteric channels, I have managed to glean certain facts and certain information in this direction that offer tasty reading. I herewith present my findings:

1. The male members of three of these censorship boards — there are state boards at the present time in

New York, Maryland, Virginia, Ohio, Kansas, Pennsylvania, and for Sunday films, in Massachusetts — found nothing particularly dirty in such words and phrases as "naked," "twin beds," "mistress," "birth control" and "long, lonely nights," but were compelled to demand their deletion upon the insistence of women members of the boards.

2. It was the women on the boards of two state censorship bodies who, against the male members' indifference, forced the elimination from certain films of such innocent spectacles as women's underclothing hanging on a clothes line and a husband appearing in his wife's presence clad in his undershirt and B.V.D.'s.

3. The deletion of such childishly harmless lines as "I wonder if Molly's mother has told her everything" (spoken by the husband on his wedding night), as "You made her so dizzy she had to go in and lie down" (spoken after a kiss), as "I'm from America" — "What part?" — "All of me," as "If you think Americans are good at the Black Bottom, just watch those Africans," and as "Come in, young man, don't be frightened. It's much warmer here than on the balcony," was ordered not by male committee members but by female.

4. Although the male censors could not discern anything excessively foul in a view of a nude little baby, of a girl sitting on a couch with a man's head in her lap, of a man in pajamas, of a girl drawing her feet up on a bench, of nightgowns arranged on a bed, of a nude figure

carved on a pipe, and of table book-ends showing a female figure's single nude breast, the women censors apparently could.

5. The censorship ladies also saw something extremely filthy in the following lines: " Corinne thinks a mistress is something you read about in a French novel "; " You know, experience should have taught you, my dear, that the name Smith is always suspicious on the hotel register "; " You mustn't think of the man in me, only the artist "; " It wasn't love "; " What's your name? " — " Eve " — " Mine's Adam "; " Is friend husband out of town again? "; and " This girl, painted as a harlot, met death with a smile."

Under beautiful rose-beds, it would seem, there are often sewers.

ᖇ ᖇ

Critical Contemplation of Man's Estate. — In every bachelor's life there comes, I suppose, a time when he weighs the theoretical enchantments of his celibacy against the theoretical enchantments of blissful matrimony. There perhaps never has existed a bachelor in full possession of all his faculties who has not, at least once, thus meditated the relative advantages and disadvantages of his estate, any more than there ever has existed a husband who has not in turn at least once — to be generous about it — meditated the relative advantages and disadvantages of his. As to a husband's secret conclusions, I have no knowledge; I can only guess. But with a bachelor's, I have a somewhat more substantial acquaintance.

When I speak of a bachelor, I speak not of one upon whom bachelorhood has been arbitrarily forced by one thing or another — lack of money, deficient biological health, responsibilities to parents, or something of the kind — but of one who is a bachelor of his own volition and by preference. Surveying himself, what does such a one imagine that he finds?

He imagines that he finds, first of all, that he is a free agent. He may do as he desires; he may go as he wills; nobody interferes with him; his time is his own; he is, in a word, his own lord and master. But is he? Contrary to his philosophical conviction that nobody interferes with him, *everybody* considers it his privilege to interfere with him. A married man may go home, lock the door, and stay there comparatively undisturbed. The world recognizes him as one withdrawn from it, as into a sanctuary. But a bachelor is anybody's prey. Being unattached and free, he must suffer the penalty of unattachment and freedom. His peace may be — and is — constantly invaded and violated by invitations from people, who " won't take no for an answer," to fill out dinner tables that he doesn't want to fill out; by telephone calls at any and all times of the night; by the intermittent dropping in upon him of all sorts and conditions of his friends; by the excessive friendliness of females for whom he has small use but who discern in him either possible altar bait or, at the worst, a free dinner; by his married male friends who, the moment their wives go to visit their mothers, pounce upon him as a combination drinking partner and guide to the night life of the city; in short, by a whole corps of individuals and incidents that a married man is never bothered with.

But even if the bachelor happens actually to be a more or less undisturbed, free and unpestered agent, does he relish his freedom so greatly and so undeviatingly as fiction and legend allege? It is the peculiarity of man that he seeks not freedom but prisons. He believes, true enough, that what he wants above everything else is freedom; he believes that, to achieve it, he would lay down his very life; but once he has got it, he begins casting about him for ways to lose it. If he is a bachelor with all the freedom in the world, it isn't many years before he has volitionally curtailed that freedom in one or more ways. He either buys or leases a house or flat that anchors him to a degree, quite as his married brother, through force of matrimonial circumstance, similarly, if to a somewhat greater degree, anchors himself. He indulges himself in amorous contacts, theoretically casual and without chains, that are often as binding as holy matrimony, and that sometimes last not only as long as the average marriage does these days, but longer. He must remember twenty birthdays where a married man may content himself with remembering but one or two and not be criticized in the least for his remission. He must exert himself to be charming to many women where a married man may confine his exertion to one. He must know the best restaurants, the best dancing places, the best theatres, whereas a married man may safely and satisfactorily express a complete ignorance of them, since, being hypothetically a homebody, it is not expected of him that he know such things. He must, in a word, be the married man's gay, worldly and experienced other self, ready at a moment's call to serve in one way or another the place the latter has left vacant in society.

The theory that there is complete happiness in freedom is a theory maintained chiefly by men who have lost their freedom. A man is seldom happy with what he has, whatever it may be, whether freedom or thraldom. Among my closest friends there have been three absolutely free men, as freedom goes. The three were bachelors, well-to-do, sound in health, successful in work, popular, and externally — in the eyes of the world — happy men. One was an artist; one was a figure in social life; one was one of the most successful of American playwrights. Within the last half-dozen years, the first shot himself, the second shot himself, and the third drowned himself on the Riviera. As all three were conspicuous figures in their different phases of activity, it is not necessary for me to make more graphic my point by mentioning their names; they are doubtless readily identifiable. "The longings and vague hopes of men, their need and craving to adore. . . ."

It is not marriage as marriage that therefore finds practical objection in the mind of the bachelor. He sees in it many merits that are missing from bachelorhood. His objection to it, rather, is a purely philosophical one. Marriage, he figures out to himself — whether correctly or incorrectly we will not argue — is a matter of defeat in one direction or another. It marks the triumph of custom and tradition over initiative, imagination and resolution. It marks the triumph of sentiment and more often sentimentality over rationality and realism. It marks a surrender of personality, a capitulation to a stronger and more determined will, however much the latter may shrewdly and persuasively masquerade in weakness and helplessness.

Viewing matrimony sometimes so sympathetically that he alarms himself with the suspicion that he himself may some day surprisingly embrace it, the bachelor yet retains sufficient calm judicially to appraise its deficiencies. In the first place, the bachelor who marries takes upon himself the responsibility for another's happiness which, in view of the fact that he has not been able to make anything like a perfect job of his own happiness, is much like asking a cripple to carry another cripple across an endless expanse of quicksands. In the second place, the bachelor is frightened by the monotony of married life, for, whatever may be said by him or others against his own life, it is at its worst hardly so monotonous as that of a married man. It is less given to routine, to adventureless humdrum.

The bachelor does not always believe that the opposite in his case leads to a particularly thrilling existence, but he realizes that, whatever the facts, he is blessed with that round-the-corner hope of something exciting that is a mortal's divinest gift. Around the corner there may be nothing at all for him, but he is in the advantageous position of not knowing it for a certainty and hence may find pleasure in mere anticipation. In the third place, the bachelor weighs the old charge against him of selfishness. Meditating it, he concludes that it is nonsense and that the really selfish man is the man who marries. There is no gainsaying the fact that, in the general run of things, the married man's well-being and physical comfort are better looked after than the bachelor's; even the least successful marriage gives a man, while it lasts, a greater share of such well-being and physical comfort than the bachelor enjoys. Yet the bachelor, duly appreciating it, unselfishly sacrifices it to his higher philosophical principles.

Nor is it a matter of selfishness so far as finances go, the bachelor ruminates. The bachelor — as any bachelor can tell you — has to spend considerably more money on women than a married man has to spend on his wife. Assuming that both men have exactly the same amount of money, it is the bachelor, not the married man, who suffers the greater expenditure. And if laying out such money on the part of the bachelor is selfishness and on the part of the married man unselfishness, considering the basic texture of the motivating emotions involved, he would like to have some married man explain the reason for the difference to him.

There is the argument, as well, that the bachelor avoids his duty to mankind and to society. Bosh. If the argument has children in mind, it may be replied that thousands upon thousands of married men equally avoid their duty to the future of the race and to society, and are thus of a piece with as many bachelors. It is the question of the relative values of matrimony and bachelorhood that we are engaging, not the well-being of society. It is the question of individual values, not mass.

Another staggerer for the bachelor is the unnecessary but inevitable external encumbrances that marriage would impose upon him. If he could marry an orphan without a relative in the world, the idea of matrimony would not be so formidable to him. But, alas, there are few such orphans and those that there are are none too alluring, and consequently he envisages himself married not only to the fair lady of his choice but to a troop of considerably less fair relatives. The thought is terrifying.

Divorce, so rapidly on the increase, is often a testimonial to the aloof wisdom of the bachelor.

In the disquisition that we have here conducted, it should be remembered that we have been discussing not the bachelor clod or the married clod but the bachelor and the married man possessed of some sensitiveness and imagination. The bachelor of this species finds that marriage would take from him an independence that he does not always want, as the married man of this species finds that marriage gives him a security that he does not always want. The bachelor sometimes looks ahead into the years and wipes away a self-pitying tear over his forlorn and lonely death, as the married man sometimes looks ahead into the years and wipes away a self-pitying tear over his too closely attended and affection-harbored life. The bachelor sees in marriage not necessarily the death of a particular illusion — an epigram out of the mouths of sophomores — but the curtailment of all those other old outside illusions that keep a man foolishly and happily and gayly young; the married man sees in his lost bachelorhood what he knows perfectly well was not there, but what, even as the bachelor vainly seeking the truth in illusion, he likes to believe was there.

It is, as we see, simply a matter of faith. If the bachelor believes in the virtues of bachelorhood, why disillusion him? If the married man believes in the virtues of matrimony, why in turn disillusion him? " There's enough unhappiness in the world as it is."

CHAPTER VII

The Sex Appeal Fiction

❧ ❧

Nothing impresses me as being quite so idiotic as the popularly held theory that this or that particular young woman's success on the stage or motion picture screen is due to her sex appeal. That she may have sex appeal in a certain direction is entirely probable, but that it has more than the slightest fraction to do with any success she achieves seems to me to be excessively dubious.

Sex appeal is more often a handicap than an asset to an actress. Consider the stage. The relatively younger actresses who currently attract the biggest audiences into the theatres are Katharine Cornell, Eva Le Gallienne, Ina Claire, Helen Hayes and Lynn Fontanne. Yet not even the greatest admirer of them or of their talents would argue that any of them is especially gifted with sex appeal. On the other hand, not even the least admirer or greatest skeptic as to the talents of such other relatively younger actresses as Miriam Hopkins, Dorothy Hall, Judith Anderson, Katharine Hepburn, Jean Arthur, Mady Christians and Erin O'Brien-Moore — allowing for the widest catholicity of taste and opinion — would argue, in turn, that they haven't considerably more of sex appeal than the ladies in the first group. Yet, while absence of sex appeal in the case of this first group hasn't interfered in the least with their audience success, presence of sex appeal in the case of the second hasn't helped the young women in it in the least. In certain specific instances, indeed, it has been something of a handicap, as it has diverted attention from the abilities of the young ladies in question and centred it upon their animal magnetism, which hasn't done them a bit of good so far as their stage careers go.

Furthermore, let us not hear that it is purely a matter of greater talent with the actresses in the first group as opposed to those in the second. The point is that, however talented Judith Anderson, an experienced actress, or Jean Arthur, a comparatively inexperienced one, may be or may become, the fact of their sex appeal is and will continue to be dinned into the public consciousness at the expense of their talent and will thus convert them into women first and actresses afterward. Whereas Miss Cornell and Miss Le Gallienne are permitted to be actresses and are discussed impersonally as actresses, these other girls are doomed to be discussed personally — and woe betide them when eventually, whatever their histrionic skill, the quality of sex appeal, with advancing years, leaves them.

In the films, it is the same. An Edna May Oliver will outlast any half-dozen Jean Harlows.

The history of the modern stage reminds us that the actresses who have exercised the greatest draught with audiences have seldom been cursed with the attribute of physical invocation. In France today, Frenchmen will assure you that the only exception to the rule is Yvonne Printemps. In England today, Englishmen will assure you that there isn't a single exception to the rule. In Germany, up to the time of Hitlerian obstruction, Elisabeth Bergner, one of the few actresses on the stage of that country who weighed under one hundred and fifty pounds, was by common German consent the one exception.

Reflect on the motion pictures. The greatest success on the screen in its earlier days was Mary Pickford, who certainly was not sought out by countless male fans for any quality of sexual stimulation. The emphasis in Miss Pickford's case was, even in the instance of the press department, distinctly in an opposite direction, culminating in the nursery-like slogan, " America's sweetheart." Even today, at forty-odd, this same Miss Pickford has attracted larger fan audiences on personal appearance tours than any more youthful sex-appeal film actress. At the present moment, perhaps the most widely popular woman screen player is Greta Garbo, a woman with youth far behind her whose sex appeal, so far as male audiences go, is largely nil and the admiration of whom lies chiefly amongst women fans. In the whole history of motion pictures, silent or audible, there is not one actress noted for her sexual attraction to men who has lasted as a considerable favorite with the fans. The Theda Baras, Louise Glaums, Clara Kimball Youngs and Dorothy Daltons flame for a period, flicker out and die. So do the Clara Bows, Harlows, del Rios and Marlene Dietrichs. The women with less sexual drive flourish much longer.

The reason probably is not far to seek. Once let a woman be told that sex appeal is her strong asset and she will spend the time in cultivating and furthering it that other women will spend in cultivating and furthering their acting talent. (Or, in personal life, their intelligence, and ability to sew, cook and keep house.) The result is that an honest career on the stage or screen is foolishly sacrificed to an evanescent one. For an actress, when youth and loveliness and sex halloo are gone, must be an actress if she wishes to draw and hold trade, not a memento of anatomical gravity. The box-office is dead for the ecstaticæ of day before yesterday.

Sex appeal, in general, is something pretty difficult to define. The late Florenz Ziegfeld, more uniformly successful in projecting girls at an audience than any American musical show producer of his time, believed that it lay in concealment, in visual cleanness and daintiness, and in a veneer of innocence — and he practised what he preached in the stage presentation of his houris. Other producers — Earl Carroll, for example — believe that it lies not in concealment but in the more or less complete revelation of the female body. They have not succeeded fully with their audiences as Ziegfeld did. George Lederer, one of the most successful showmen before Ziegfeld, believed that it consisted largely in a girl's carriage — and addressed himself to making his young women comport themselves like so many undulating wienerwursts. George Edwardes, England's most successful producer of musical comedy at the famous old Gaiety, believed, on the contrary, that it consisted in not having the girls move at all, or at best as little as possible. In other words, to have them stand still and not allow movement to interrupt the static picture. Pay your money and take your choice of these various philosophies.

But sex appeal, other persons believe, may conceivably dismiss the eye altogether. The voice of an unknown woman over the telephone has often, for some, carried with it a deal of sexual sorcery. So with the radio, as witness the reaction to the singing voice of Frances Langford.

The whole matter, indeed, presents a peculiar problem. What is sex appeal to one man is often an ice-poultice to another. To believe that any single young woman possesses an inflammatory appeal to men in the mass is to believe that all men — or, in any event, the majority of men — are cut-outs from the same emotional pattern and respond equally and alike to exactly the same stimulus. This, obviously, is nonsense. If you need convincing, reflect upon the extreme dissimilarity of the women various men admire. Take a look at their best girls. Or at their wives.

A young woman in private life may have this quality of sex appeal for certain males of her acquaintance. Yet, even here, their number is limited. If, among the young women you, the reader, know personally you can decide upon *one* who exercises an equal amount of anatomical magnetism upon all or even the majority of your male acquaintances, I shall freely confess to the weakness of my contention. But I have a feeling that you cannot. The best you will probably be able to do will be to hit upon one or maybe two girls who have a biologically electrical effect upon yourself and perhaps several of your male friends, but as for their effect upon the great number of other men whom you know you will either have to rely on pretty doubtful guess-work or simply, puzzled and confounded, shake your head. Therefore, the notion that any one young woman on the stage or screen, however ooh-hoo, can exercise a sexually bewitching influence upon *countless* audiences of men hardly holds water, save to sentimental nitwits.

Sex appeal to one man may consist in a woman's figure. But what that man considers a good figure, another man may consider, in his prejudice, not at all a good figure. Some men admire curves and plumpness; others, slenderness and straight lines. The same thing holds true in the case of big eyes or small slanted ones, in the case of brashness and sophistication on the one hand or artless innocence on the other, and in the case of contralto or soprano vocal tones. What is one man's meat is another man's poison. Take, for example, two women who are alleged to have succeeded in the motion pictures — and succeeded with the same kind of large audiences — principally because of their sex appeal, to wit, Mae West and Constance Bennett. While we are asked to believe that both of these girls have stimulated the same masculine audiences in the same way, a moment's reflection is sufficient to emphasize the fact that both are totally and wholly unalike in every particular. One is loud and brash, the other quiet and moderately withdrawn. One is of a voluptuous shape, the other of a slim, almost boyish shape. One speaks like a bartender, the other like a high-school girl. One goes directly at men hammer and tongs; the other approaches them from around the corner. There are still other differences. Yet both are said to triumph over the same men because of their sex appeal. Sex appeal probably has no more to do with it than Janet Gaynor's lack of what is thus designated as sex appeal has to do with *her* popular success.

Sex appeal is that loosely defined element in a young woman's makeup that appeals to certain men. The element in question often has very little connection with sex. The sex appeal is really an after-thought. A man likes the way a girl moves, or casts her eyes, or does her hair, or purses her lips, or sits down, or stands up — and then concludes that she has sexual attraction. The latter, to him, is really the residuum of *sentimental* attraction. It begins as heart appeal and then subsequently is transmuted into sex appeal. And men's cardiac susceptibilities are as various as their sexual.

If sex appeal, as it is commonly known, were as simple a matter as some believe, that is, merely physical stimulation, the burlesque houses with their "living pictures" and "strippers" would have a monopoly on the eager masculine trade. The fact that they are very far from having any such monopoly goes to prove that what draws men into the amusement halls, whether dramatic, music show or film, is not a seeking after physical excitation but a seeking after romantic — or, in the instance of more adult minds — humorous excitation.

"What does he see in her?" has been in the language from time immemorial, and its deathlessness attests to the diversity of men's tastes and reactions, sexual as well as otherwise. The theory that the moment men enter a theatre or a movie parlor they abandon all differences of attitude and feeling toward women and suddenly find that one particular woman gives them simultaneously and equally an enormous anatomical kick is, I fear, what our less literary critics describe as hooey. The kick they really get is a sentimental one, but — being men — they chestily like to pretend that it is something different.

CHAPTER VIII

O'Neill

ல ல

Since my early critical interest, many years ago, in his work, there has persisted a legend that my close friendship with and personal affection for him have induced in me a critical astigmatism as to his defects as a dramatist. The legend is gifted with such blood-pressure, indeed, that so recently as a year past another friend of his, in the flow of a discourse that agitated the tall palms outside his library window on that island off the Georgia coast, delivered himself of the opinion that my constant and unremitting endorsement of O'Neill had done him more harm than good, inasmuch as it had in all likelihood — for such is sometimes the peculiar critical reaction — prejudiced other commentators against him. Upon the friend's oracularity, O'Neill himself ventured nothing, merely — as is his wont when a view on almost any subject is desired or expected of him — contenting himself in slowly dredging himself up from the depths of his chair, moving at snail's pace to a distant cigarette box, laboriously extracting therefrom a cigarette, and consuming at least three minutes in the lighting of it and meditating the flavor of his initial puff.

His fair wife, Carlotta, however, let out a whoop. " Endorsement! " she fulminated. " Constant endorsement! " she went on. " What do you mean? Did you read his unspeakable reviews of ' Dynamo '? I hadn't met him then, but I said to myself, ' Anyone who could be that nasty and unfair to Gene, dismissing a whole play in terms of a mere lengthy cataloguing of exaggerated stage directions, would never be allowed within even hailing distance of me.' Then what of the unholy ridicule he poured on ' Welded,' and what of his abrupt dismissal of ' The First Man '? What, too, of his criticism of ' Lazarus Laughed '? Why, the fellow even found fault with one or two things about ' Mourning Becomes Electra,' which even the critics most hostile to Gene praised whole-heartedly! "

I take the impolite liberty of quoting Mrs. O'Neill's denunciation of my occasional critical attitude toward her husband because it constitutes a much politer exculpation of a professional critic than any such critic might, within the precise bounds of professional taste, vouchsafe to himself.

One of the irritations that beset the critic is the common imputation to him of motives of one sort or another. It is generally believed, for example, that the critic cannot be the friend of a man and yet view him and his work impersonally. The closer the friendship, the more — so goes the conviction — is it likely that the critic will be drawn toward arbitrary praise. It is assumed, in other words, that not only is the critic himself a half-wit but that he is in the invariable habit of picking out only half-wits for intimate friends. That friendship may follow, rather than precede, work ably and soundly done, that it may be based upon mutual respect and a regard for personal integrity and honor, and that any invasion or corruption of any one of these would immediately end it, is apparently overlooked. O'Neill probably does not relish my periodic dispraise of his dramatic writings any more than I, in turn, relish his periodic impatience with and dispraise of my critical writings, but that does not interfere with a decent friendship.

I have been reading his plays in advance manuscript form for, now, something like sixteen years and, sometimes, long before they have seen the light of theatrical performance, have expressed my favorable or unfavorable opinion of them to him. He has sulked on occasion, has even called me a damned fool, when we have differed, but it has meant no more to him than it has to me when, for instance, upon reading the advance manuscript of one of my recent books, he has expressed a very decidedly unfavorable opinion of it and I, in turn, have called him a damned fool. We are, I suppose, friends for better or worse, till the water-wagon or continued bad work in the case of either doth us part, and that — disturbing as it may be to some — is that.

When I started to confect this chapter on him, I had an inclination to give it the title, "The New O'Neill." I refrained for the reason that, though the O'Neill of today is a considerably changed man from the O'Neill I have known in past years, no man ever really changes so greatly as to warrant any such absurd politico-journalistic caption. Yet that there has been a change in the old O'Neill is unmistakable.

When I first knew him, back in the earlier Nineteen Hundreds, he exuded all the gay warmth of an Arctic winter. To say that he was a melancholy, even a morbid, fellow is to put it mildly. Life to him in those days — and not only life but his stock-taking of his own soul — was indistinguishable from a serial story consisting entirely of bites from mad dogs, fatal cancers and undertakers disappointed in love. His look suggested a man who was just about to guzzle a vase of $C_{33}H_{45}No_{12}$, and his conversation suggested a man who *had* guzzled it. In addition, he was chronically so nervous and physically so restive that he generally gave one the impression, what with his constant sharp, jerky glances to the left and right, that he was imminently on the worried look-out for the police. When he took hold of a highball glass, his hand shook so that he sounded like a Swiss bell ringer. In the last four years he has regained a calm and tranquillity of such proportions that their very *adagissimo* induces in one all the nervousness and restiveness that used to be his. Nothing any longer disturbs or remotely agitates him. He is at peace with himself and with the world.

One of the greatest recent changes that has come over him, however, is a recapture of the humor that was in him in those distant days before even he began to write, in the days that I have described in the volume called " The Intimate Notebooks of George Jean Nathan," when, at the dives known as Jimmy the Priest's and the Hell Hole, where he made his residence, he was part and parcel of such low buffoonery as has seldom been chronicled in the biography of *homo literarum Americanus*. There was a long period when humor and the O'Neill drama were strangers — the period when he himself was in the spiritual, mental and physical dumps — although even then, despite the seeming skepticism of his critics, there were occasional fleeting symptoms of that grim humor which was in him in the old, previous days and which was struggling pathetically and often baffled to come again to the surface. But the new O'Neill humor is not a grim humor; it is a kindly and gentle and often very tender humor, wholly unlike any that has fitfully edged its way into even those of his plays that have not been abruptly catalogued by his critics as " morbid," " gloomy," " lugubrious," or what not. Much of his prospective work must surely testify to the fact.

As one of his critics, I have never been one, incidentally, to be persuaded that O'Neill's drama is exactly what the majority of his commentators have professed to regard it, to wit, a drama almost uniformly bereft of any and all traces of humor. There have been plays, of course, as noted, that have been — and properly — as devoid of humor as Bach's passacaglio in C minor or a toothache, but there assuredly have been others — before the admitted " Ah, Wilderness! " — that have contained some very genuine humor, whatever qualifying adjective doubtful critics may elect to attach to it. " Marco Millions " is fundamentally and in the aggregate a humorous play; " Desire Under the Elms " has plain shots of sardonic humor; the beginning of " The Emperor Jones " is tickled with a humorous straw; there is open-and-shut humor in some of the early sea one-acters; and there are glints of humor here and there in other scripts. To argue that O'Neill has not had humor because a lot of it has been of the grim variety is to argue, on the same ground, that neither had Chekhov any.

Another change in O'Neill is a mood of optimism and faith that has supplanted his old, indurated pessimism and disillusion. Where formerly his outlook on life and on himself was generally glum and bitter, there is in him now evidence of a measure of philosophical rosiness and trust. As his personal life has been eased with solicitude and affection and faith, his mind, once cramped and clouded, has perceptibly mellowed and brightened. He is not yet a gay fellow by any means, for it is not in his born nature to be gay, but compared with his previous self he is a veritable hornpipe. Life and the world and the agonies of humanity are still, of course, a source of much brow-wrinkling for him, and not a little meditative pain, but back of it all one can vaguely hear a tune singing in his heart. Speaking of tunes, by the way, his last year's greatest desire was to install in his house one of those old-time saloon-bordello pianos that were operated by dropping a nickle into them and whose façades, immediately the nickle was deposited, burst into a magnificent illumination. Such a proud musical instrument he has succeeded, after six months' assiduous search, in locating.

〜 〜

O'Neill is the hardest worker that I have ever known, and, in the roster of my writing acquaintances, I have known a number of pretty hard workers. There isn't a minute of the day that his thoughts are not in some way or another on his work. Even when sound asleep, his wife informs me, he will once in a while grunt and be heard to mumble something about Greek masks, Freudian psychology, or Philip Moeller. Not so long ago, swimming with him after two hours in what seemed to me to be waters still at least sixty dreadful miles from the safe Georgia shore, and with both our stomachs full of wet salt, he turned over on his back for a moment, ejected a good part of the Atlantic Ocean from his mouth and told me that he had just been thinking it over and had decided to change one of the lines in his second act. I have eaten, drunk, walked, motored, bicycled, slept, bathed, shaved, edited, run, worked, played, even sung with him, and it has been a rare occasion, take my word for it, when he has not interrupted whatever we were doing to venture this or that observation on this or that manuscript he was then busied upon. He may be reading the morning newspaper, or studying the Washington financial letter service to which he subscribes, or lying half-asleep on the beach, or fishing for pompano, or gobbling a great bowl of chop suey, or hugging his wife, or openly envying some new-fangled sport shirt you may happen to be wearing, or making a wry face over Dreiser's poetry, or doing anything else under God's sun, but you may be sure that what he is thinking about all the time and turning over in his mind is something concerned with his playwriting.

A dozen times a day he will stop in the middle of a sentence and, without a word of apology or explanation, depart, head dejected, to his writing room to make note of a line or an idea that has just occurred to him. He has, at the present moment, notebooks full of enough dramatic themes, dialogue and what not to fill all the theatres in New York for the next twenty years, with sufficient material left over to fill most of those in London, Paris, and Stockholm. I not long ago asked him about two or three rather fully developed ideas for plays that he had told me of a few years before at Le Plessis, in France, where he was then living. " Oh, I don't think I'll ever do anything about them," he allowed. " I've got a couple of dozen or so new ones I begin to like better."

O'Neill's chief professional concern in more recent years has been the problem of casting his plays to his own satisfaction. The dearth of good actors, principally in the male department, causes him no end of anxiety. So much, indeed, that not long ago he confided to me that his ambition, once he gets enough money to be safe, is not to permit his future plays to be produced but simply to publish them, uncorrupted by careless and obfuscating acting, in book form. "You can say what you want to about the theatre back in my old man's time," he held forth; "you can laugh at all those tin-pot plays and all that, but, by God, you've got to admit that the old man and all the rest of those old boys were *actors!*"

∽ ∽

The re-birth of the old O'Neill humor, to which I have alluded, has been made amply evident in "Ah, Wilderness!" Here we have a photographically true comedy of a thoroughly recognizable American household of the early Nineteen Hundreds dipped in the developing acids of a sure, sympathetic and amused dramatic imagination. There will be some, I take it, who — still laboring under the critical superstition that what makes one smile, and smiling chortle, can never be as important as what makes one feel cousin to a grave-digger — will assign the play to an inferior position in the catalogue of its author's accomplishments. But this selfsame play seems to one who doesn't feel quite that way to be one of the best, one of the most humanly deep, and one of the most heart-filled things that O'Neill has written — even if, as the fact is, he tossed it off in a month's time.

For the last ten years it has been the local critical patois that George Kelly is first and foremost in the dramatic treatment of such homely family materials as " Ah, Wilderness! " contains. As one critic, I have never been able to share my colleagues' uniform opinion as to Mr. Kelly's great virtues. That he has some virtues, and of a very definite kind, is readily to be allowed; but that, as a dramatist in his chosen field, he has bulked as large as his friendly commentators have insisted, I have never been able to get myself to believe. I find some little satisfaction, as a consequence, in the fact that in " Ah, Wilderness! " O'Neill has written not only what falls into the reviewers' pigeonhole as " a George Kelly play," but that at the same time he has showed Kelly and his endorsing critics just what a so-called Kelly play should really be.

The story, as has been noted, of a typical American family of some twenty-five or -six years ago, the play pretty well justifies its folk comedy sub-title. There is not a character in it that isn't more or less familiar in retrospect to almost anyone who lived in and knew that period. Here and there, there is a slight touch of exaggeration, but such touches only point the integrity of the characters the more. To the whole, there is a family album and old tin-type quality that is unmistakable. There is a bit of every now grown-up boy's father in that stage's father, as there is a bit of every such boy's mother, and uncle, and brothers and sisters. There is also a hint of every such boy's first love affair, and of his first timid adventure in sin, and of his first brave, manly struggle with alcoholic liquor. That autobiography has figured in the O'Neill record is as certain as that it figures in the audience's memory.

It has come as a surprise to many that O'Neill had it in him to write such an amusing comedy; one containing as many legitimate loud theatre laughs as any first-rate comedy by a professional comedy writer seen hereabouts in some time. (In order to fit the play into the usual theatre time, indeed, it was necessary for O'Neill to cut out twenty-four minutes of laughs which unduly invaded his main story.) Why it should be a surprise, I don't know. It is beside the point to repeat that in certain of O'Neill's antecedent work we have had evidence of his humor. But it is less beside the point to call attention again to the silly idea that, because a dramatist writes gravely on grave topics, he must arbitrarily be devoid of the comic gift. They thought it, in his time, of Björnson, and for more than twenty years, until he proved to them that they were fools. They thought it of Hauptmann until, disgusted, he quickly seized them by their donkey ears and gave them a couple of first-rate comedies within a period of eleven months. They thought it of Synge until he made them unbelieving of their own eyes at the spectacle of " The Playboy of the Western World." They are always thinking it.

In this play O'Neill has abandoned temporarily his avid experimenting with complex new dramatic forms and has worked in the simplest and most forthright. I am glad to observe the happy and eminently satisfactory result, for it seems to me that there is sometimes a dogmatic and faintly strained effort on his part to evolve a new and strange dramatic form where the more conventional and established form would not only serve his immediate purpose just as well but even, perhaps, a little better. After all, when all is said and done, most of the fine plays of the modern theatre are found to have been written in the simplest manner.

We now turn to less pleasant news.

Those critical spirits in our midst who contend that, not O'Neill, but everyone else from Mr. Robert Sherwood to the Hattons is the first dramatist of the American theatre will find great comfort in O'Neill's most recent play, "Days Without End," which is not only, along with "Welded" and "Dynamo," one of the poorest things he has written but which, in addition, is one of the dullest that has come to the more ambitious stage in some time. Further comfort, if it be needed, will be afforded them in the undeniable fact that it is one of the most unbroiled plays that has been composed upon its general theme. And to make matters worse for those of us who believe in O'Neill's very considerable talent and better for those who don't, the fellow actually considers it the best play he has ever written!

From beginning to end, save for two brief flashes, this "Days Without End" is a tournament in collegiate theorizing artlessly bamboozled into a superficial aspect of grave experimental drama by a recourse to masks and to the technical device — favorite of German, Austrian, and Hungarian playwrights like Von Scholtz and Molnár in the years before the war — of co-ordinating the narration of a hypothetical fiction story with the actual lives of the immediate characters. It comes to the old tale: when O'Neill goes in for pure emotion, he is a sound and enormously effective dramatist; but when he ventures into theorizing and philosophizing, he is — to be very gallant about it — far from palatable. In the present play, he had a play of pure emotion, exalted emotion even. But every time it pops up its head he gives it a mortal clout with a pseudo-ratiocinative bladder. The result is chaos — and tedium.

"Days Without End," a reconstruction of the Faust idea (with Faust and Mephistopheles imagined as one) and seeking its resolution under the Cross of the Catholic Christ, cries piteously for a poetry that is nowhere in it. Its lines are not only banal and humdrum, but — worse — at certain moments when only the high and thrilling beauty of the written English word might bring it a second's exaltation, the author descends to such gross argot as "Forgive me for butting in" and the like. The net final impression is of a crude religious tract liberally sprinkled with a lot of dated Henry Arthur Jones sex in an effort

[124]

to give it a feel of theatrical life. O'Neill sub-titles his play,
" a modern miracle play." It is not modern, as he himself
should realize, since he originally wrote it with the scene
set back something like fifty years. And, if he knows the
miracle plays, which he most assuredly does, he certainly
realizes that this forced, tortured and hocus-pocused slice
of greasepaint drama is anything but a miracle play in the
sense of such a play's cool simplicity, and innocence, and
moving dignity.

In this work of his, O'Neill — as in other of his un-
successful theorizing matches — again suggests a bulldog
ferociously battling a Haldeman-Julius Little Blue Book.
It shows nothing of the cold, hard, calm critical gift which,
paradoxically enough, he exercises upon his unadulterated
emotional plays. In place of that cold self-criticism, which
has provided our American stage with some of its finest
plays, we find here an intoxication with what may be
called logicalized emotionalism, which turns out to be
neither logic nor emotion but only a bogus Siamese twin.
The passion that should have gone into the play's emotional and spiritual fabric is spent upon what the author
evidently cherishes as a sacrosanct amorous ethic, an ethic
that seems more and more dubious as his passion continues indignantly to inflame and apotheosize it. Aiming
at a climactic exaltation of the spirit, he succeeds infinitely
less in accomplishing his purpose than whoever the play-
carpenter was who years ago made the honky-tonk version
of " Faust " for Lewis Morrison and brought his final

curtain down on Mephistopheles' bafflement and frustration by having the tin covering fall loudly off a cross atop a church and having the cross suddenly illuminated, like an old Shubert chorus, with a lot of very dazzling and embarrassingly pink electric bulbs.

"Days Without End" may be a testimonial to O'Neill's newly found optimism, but it is hardly one to his older gift for sound dramatic writing.

CHAPTER IX

Summer Theatres

The dramatic hot-dog stands commonly known as summer theatres have for the last few years been in profuse bloom throughout the eastern American countryside. I haven't the exact figures at hand, but a perusal of the warm weather newspapers indicates that in almost every rural section boasting a filling station with more than one pump you will find at least one such wayside shrine to the Muse. The great majority of these shrines, as the reader is already sufficiently aware, started out in life not as playhouses but as residences of cows, roller-skating rinks, town halls, manure sheds, garages, or something equally alien to the purple art of sock and buskin. Their wholesale conversion began about three years ago, and their wholesale re-conversion will in all likelihood begin about three years hence.

It isn't that, here and there, you will not find one such little summer theatre that serves a purpose other than gratifying the vanity of some young man who imagines himself enormously gifted in the craft of production and stage direction and who yet hasn't been able to get past the astutely critical office-boys of the New York managers. It is, rather, that most of the theatres — and by far the most — are simply repetitions of the more jitney Broadway theatres, and so are without rhyme or reason in the scheme of things reputably theatrical. So far as imagination, experimentation or fresh judgment goes, they are dead from the chin up. They are merely ineffectual little cuckoos of the parrot cages of Broadway. They discover nothing genuine in the way of playwriting talent, directorial talent, or acting talent. They believe that they deserve their place in the sun if they so much as uncover, in combination, a few second-rate plays by third-rate hacks that subsequently get some money at the New York box-office. They strive neither courageously nor honestly, but rest content to be so many mimics of zeros.

How, then, do they manage to persist? They manage to persist because their operators succeed in hornswoggling a lot of poor young actors, starved for a sniff of fresh country air, to sweat through the summer weeks at Chinese coolie wages; because these same operators make a magnanimous show of trying out inferior plays by inferior playwrights and offering their magnanimity in lieu of cash royalties; and because the neighbors exhaust the little film house programs (changed but twice a week) in two nights and seem to have nothing better to do on another night in the week than to patronize the local converted horsehouse, it being a notorious and well-appreciated fact that nothing on this earth is so entirely and overwhelmingly boresome as living in the country for long after night-fall. (Which, incidentally, as the psychologists seem to have overlooked, is the reason at bottom for the farmers' chronic discontent and eternal dissatisfaction with their lot.)

The people who reside in the neighborhood of the little summer theatres will some day have to answer to their Maker for the sins they commit against the well-being of the art of the drama. They applaud the worst kind of dramatic rubbish; they applaud the most slovenly brand of acting; they give teas and cocktail parties for the guileless actors and actresses and tell them what wonderful artists they are; they invite the operators of the theatres to the country club and ask them their important opinions of Stanislavski, Danchenko and Reinhardt; they flatter, grease, oil and gush until the poor idiots of actors, actresses and producers idiotically imagine themselves wows of the first carat and in the autumn descend upon New York brave and bumptious in their self-unrecognized but painfully obvious incompetence.

As has been noted, not all of the summer show-shops are such affronts to decency and honor. There are a few with elements to recommend them. These deserve to live and prosper. But in the aggregate the outhouses of Thespis contrive to do infinitely more harm than good. They discourage, with their amateurish productions, cheap taste and trivial plays, winter attendance upon the reputable professional theatre. For the neighboring country customers, though they may not temporarily figure it out that way to themselves, unquestionably discover — when they take stock of their senses at the end of the summer — that the country theatre was, after all, pretty unsatisfactory and pretty unglamorous and, confusing that theatre with the winter professional theatre, conclude that they have had enough of any kind of theatre for plenty of months to come.

If, even with all their other faults, the small summer theatres served soundly as experimental stages for possibly worth-while plays and acted as intelligent laboratories for the New York theatre, they might find sympathy at the hands of criticism. But glance at their record. Out of approximately 150 new manuscripts that they tried out in 1933, what was the relative amount of wheat (if you can call it that) to chaff? The only new plays thus tried out that subsequently got anywhere on Broadway were " The Pursuit of Happiness," a box-office farce-comedy of utterly no critical importance, " Double Door," a tin-pot box-office melodrama, and " No More Ladies," a distinctly second-rate, if here and there fairly amusing, comedy. The various others that were brought to the New York stage were all trash, and were all failures. And the statistics for the year previous were even less fortunate. Out of any number of plays tried out then, three and only three were deemed fit for New York audiences. And the three that were deemed fit were the trashy " Chrysalis," Susan Glaspell's and Norman Matson's dud, " The Comic Artist," and the murder melodrama, "Nine Pine Street." All three were failures. As for 1934, the record at this writing looks to be no more promising.

Surely, therefore, the summer theatres are sheer waste in this important direction. In the last three years they haven't found one single reputable new piece of dramatic writing. In the last three years, furthermore, they haven't developed one single new stage producer of any discernible skill. In the last three years the only new actor they have uncovered is the young Teuton, Tonio Selwart — and Herr Selwart, while a good-looking lad, is no histrio to get particularly excited about. And, in the last three years they haven't found a single new young actress of more than ordinary talent. Something, quite apparently, is wrong somewhere. Maybe such an organization as the Group Theatre originally hit upon the proper solution of the problem. That solution was to go to the country, quietly rehearse a play all summer, keep theatrically mum about it, stay away from all tea and cocktail parties, and bring the play into New York, for better or worse, in the Fall. Maybe, too, even that wasn't the solution.

CHAPTER X

A Trio of Reflections

❧ ❧

Whither? — Among my minor prejudices is the word *whither* in the title of a book, play, lecture, magazine article, or essay. Anything labelled " Whither America? ", " Whither Are We Drifting? " or whither anything else finds in me a very reluctant customer. There is something in whither that evokes the picture of a sententious stuffed shirt who, given in private person to the use of where, imagines that the employment in his public manifestations of the tonier whither will invest him with a bit of gravity and literary air. Having so apologized for the title of the present inquiry, I duly pain my clients with the query: whither is the stage going in the matter of sex?

That word *sex,* incidentally, is something else that — with its touch of evasive hypocrisy — is beginning to wherret me. In private speech, of course, none of us is guilty of the polite circumlocution which it represents. Yet with the exception of perhaps a couple of young sub-Mason and Dixon novelists, one expatriated Irishman, one (deceased) expatriated Englishman, and a few bad boys from Chicago — most of them at one time or another suppressed — there is scarcely a living writer in English who does not take refuge in the ambiguous term. (Even the late Frank Harris, who was certainly no linguistic chicken-heart, had timid recourse to it to designate everything from Kamasutran calisthenics to the duct of Müller.)

Having thus apologized doubly, I restate the query: whither is the stage going in the matter of sex?, and proceed to business.

It is plainly evident that, save in a few sporadic instances, the play that deals seriously with sex in the normal aspect of the past is no longer successful in capturing the interest of audiences. The reason doubtless lies in the fact that, while the audiences are not necessarily themselves abnormal, they have wearied of the years-old dramatic reiteration of normal sex themes, and have demanded a change, if only for an evening's theatrical diversion. "The Captive" began to indicate the altered taste; and since then the statistician of the theatre has noted a steadily increasing dramatic drift toward sexual bizarrerie. So decided a drift, indeed, that one wonders what will be the end. Certainly when America's first dramatist is loudly ridiculed for attempting, in his latest play, to fashion drama out of a married man's distress induced by the fact that he has been unfaithful on one occasion to his wife; certainly when one of the foremost of our actresses is hooted off to the storehouse after only a few nights for playing the rôle of a woman who almost dies from shock when she learns that her husband has been carrying on with her maid; certainly when, with a single

exception, every play treating soberly of normal sex reactions during the same last theatrical year has been a box-
office failure — certainly then it becomes obvious that the
wind is blowing the drama's sails in a new and strange
direction. (Or perhaps simply in the old, classical one.)

The wind in point has accordingly and successfully
wafted a number of peculiarly exotic blooms to us in the
last few seasons. It has wafted "Mourning Becomes Electra," with its undertone of incest; "Design For Living,"
with its overtone of androgynous sex; "The Green Bay
Tree," with its male perversion; "Dangerous Corner,"
with its note of homosexuality; "Tobacco Road," with
is combined erotomania, incest, nymphomania, and
what not else; "Mademoiselle," with its hardly concealed
suggestion of tribadism linked with paedophilia; "For
Services Rendered," with its incidental note of combined
algolagnia, bipolarity, conversion and paralogy; etc., etc.
If things keep going in the same direction, and with the
same velocity, the sex drama of the next few years will
make the "Vatermord" of Berlin notoriety look in comparison and retrospect like "A Kiss For Cinderella."

ᔈ ᔈ

No. 2. — A second reflection on the last season brings us
to the demulcent conviction that we have now probably
had all the anti-Nazi plays that we are going to get, and
that this season will be mercifully free from evenings in
which German Jewish households (whose large nobility

and unexampled virtue are indicated by an unremitting series of paternal, maternal and filial osculations and embraces) are suddenly disturbed by the entrance of a doggy actor in a brown blouse who looks disconcertingly like Mr. Eric Von Stroheim and who — after several piercing and somewhat salivary pronouncements to the effect that the aforesaid Jewish families are vermin, swine, lice, scum, offal, dung, and various foul smells — thwacks the son across the face with his swagger-stick, kicks the old father under the library table (usually piled with Goethe, Schiller, Lessing and Vicki Baum, by way of implying the old man's subversive cultural leanings), denounces the old mother as a female Schnauzer of Jewish extraction, and — after a lascivious glance through his monocle at the blonde Aryan serving-maid — loudly commands that the entire lot, with the exception of the blonde, be out of the country within five minutes, thereupon stamping out of the house followed by several supers from the local Y.M.H.A. with swastikas on their arms.

The four anti-Nazi plays disclosed during the last season (one of them, " Races," produced by the Theatre Guild, was gratefully allowed to pass out in Philadelphia before adding to the New York agony) all pursued, with but minor deviation, the standard pattern. What other pattern, indeed, there might be for such plays is pretty hard to figure out. The father may, true enough, be a *goy* married to a Jewess, as in " The Shattered Lamp," or the ingénue may be a Jewess betrothed to a Gentile stormtrooper, as in "Birthright," or everybody may be Jews, as — if memory serves — in "Kultur," but, whatever they are, Eric Von Stroheim with his swagger-stick, monocle and swastika is dead certain to pop in at the end of the second act and do his stuff, to the accompaniment of considerable sympathetic window-pane busting and off-stage general hell-raising on the part of presumably Nazi stage-hands. After a dose or two of this routine mallarkey, it may be appreciated that any additional Nazi *opera* are hardly likely to offer much interest or stimulation, whether in one way or another. About the only possible novelty would be to show a Berlin Jewish household with Maxie Baer, Maxie Rosenbloom, Barney Ross, King Levinsky and Jack Dempsey (by his own confession partly Jewish) occupying the guest rooms and to have them come downstairs in their pajamas on the entrance of the inevitable Eric and knock his block off. This, if followed by an exhibition of fancy bag-punching, might conceivably sell a few tickets at the box-office, which would be an added novelty.

A more serious thought that occurs in connection with these theatrical anti-Nazi propaganda exhibits is that, instead of accomplishing their aim in creating sympathy for the persecuted Jews, they actually — and refractorily — often provoke in their spectators, if not exactly sympathy for, at least a trace of generous understanding of, the Nazi point of view. It is a well-known dramatic fact that the moment you make a character or characters too all-fired noble and sweet an audience will gag at them. And, as a consequence of the long local display of a run of sickening Pollyanna drama, with its emphasis on sweetness and light, it is equally a well-recalled fact that there followed — to audiences' great satisfaction — a kind of drama in which the villains of the antecedent drama were, for all their knavery, pictured fairly and honestly as being possessed of certain facets of dignity, equity, and even lovableness. The trouble with the anti-Hitler propaganda drama is that it makes all its Jews Pollyannas and all its Nazis Simon Legrees, with the result that audiences (even when largely Jewish) are nauseated by the goose-grease and are brought quietly to allow to themselves that the Nazis cannot, after all, be quite so bad as the playwrights paint them. If dramatists wish to manufacture anti-Nazi plays that will accomplish their propaganda ends, it might be well for them to ponder the reactions to the plays that have been revealed thus far. This current Hitler sardoodledom will never get them anywhere. Surely not *all* the quiet, intelligent, studious old family-loving Germans are Jews; there must also be at least a few such in the Nazi ranks. And surely not every German, young or old, who believes in Hitlerism is a Jack-the-Ripper. Let the playwrights show the other side as well — and then may the best team win!

∽ ∽

No. 3. — A third reflection on the last season has to do with the melancholy failure of our American so-called experimental dramatists at their own game. It would seem

[137]

to the theatrical commentator that the chief weakness of these experimental playwrights is that what they are pleased to consider more or less daring and novel experiment is, if not quite as old as the hills, at least old enough to be thoroughly familiar to even the more casual theatregoer. One often wonders, incidentally, if the boys have ever gone to the theatre in the last ten years to learn what is going on there.

Consider, for example, by the record of this last season alone, the case of O'Neill, grantedly the first among the local experimental playwrights. In "Days Without End" he presented what he imagined were two instances of fresh experiment, to wit, the use of a masked second character to indicate the other self of his first character, and the device of a story in the process of being written by the protagonist and closely identified with the latter's immediate overt acts, thoughts, fears and resolves. The first experiment has been familiar to theatregoers for more than a decade, since initially it was employed by Alice Gerstenberg in " Overtones "; and the second experiment, as hereinbefore noted, has been even better known to them for an even greater length of time through its use by Wilhelm Von Scholz in the Theatre Guild's production of "The Race With the Shadow," to say nothing of various maneuverings by Molnár, Schnitzler, *et al.* (Speaking of O'Neill, though it has nothing to do with the present case, it is odd to recall that the selfsame critics who decried him for turning dramatically from atheism to faith in " Days

Without End" praised him enthusiastically for turning from cynicism to sentiment in "Ah, Wilderness!")

Consider, secondly, John Howard Lawson, who likes to believe himself such an experimenter as hasn't been heard of in the world since Darius Green fastened a pinwheel to his proboscis, tied a bedsheet to his tail, and jumped off the barn roof in the sublime faith that he was a flying machine. Mr. Lawson's most recent great experimentation consisted — in "The Pure In Heart" — in bringing "a new mood into the realistic theatre," the aforesaid new mood being negotiated by putting some modernistic scenery on a revolving stage, chopping his acts into short scenes, causing off-stage music to be played through certain episodes, and at points in the proceedings introducing a blues singer and six Albertina Rasch dancers. With infinitely greater art and infinitely greater success, and with about twenty times as much originality and inventiveness, any number of musical show producers the world over have been doing exactly the same thing for years — and with very much better basic dramatic stories, to boot.

Consider, finally, Sidney Howard and his much-admired experimental staging technique in the case of "Yellow Jack." If, either in the way of setting, lighting or general staging, this was a new and novel experimental technique, Herr Leopold Jessner will, when and if he hears about it, be the most surprised man in or out of Germany.

CHAPTER XI

Several Writers for the Theatre — and Miss Stein

ഗ ഗ

Mr. Priestley. — For some time now it has been my conviction that my English critical colleagues, undeniably talented and handsome though a number of them are, have become somewhat spoony in the appraisal of the English plays that they are called upon to review. Freely allowing for critical differences of opinion, we have nevertheless often found that exhibits which they have enthusiastically endorsed have been the seediest sort of gimcracks, and unaccountable of endorsement or enthusiasm even had they been written by their mothers, wives or best girls. Critical difference of opinion has had nothing to do with the matter; the plays were very bad plays and there was an end to it; it was simply unbelievable that any critic, proficient or not, could manage to detect the slightest merit in them. The business could not be put down to log-rolling, for there is very little of that kind of thing among the English dramatic critics. They are, indeed, often more honest in the case of their friends — witness their frequent artillery in the direction of Shaw, to single out one instance — than in the case of complete strangers. Nor can it be put down to ignorance, for among the critics over there there is a full quota highly intelligent and very sharp-witted. Confronted in this juncture, therefore, by a loud call for the exact reason for their delinquency, I find myself taking refuge in the safe, if quite entirely unsatisfactory, answer that I'll be damned if I know.

As I have remarked in the past, only the very young or the very old dramatic critic is absolutely positive on all matters pertaining to the theatre. Each, when he beneficently endows his customers with an opinion, nails the flag to the mast and then seats himself with a triumphant and majestic certainty atop the pole. The critic of middle years, on the other hand, occasionally finds himself (much to his secret displeasure and annoyance) infected with dubitations, some of them of such refractory magnetism that they at least momentarily pull him from his complacent anchor. The English critic, whatever his years, generally gives one the impression of being in either the very young or very old critical catalogue, or simultaneously in both. There is an air of perfect finality to his decisions that permits of no shadow of doubt. He makes up not only his own mind, but everybody's else, and — for all his often urbane phraseology — with some insistence. We Americans are supposed to be over-awed and, say what you more patriotic bounders will, it is a regrettable fact that many are. For, after all, in any field, a defiant and confident positiveness usually exercises its effect upon others. A wily newsboy in a quiet side-street yelling out a bogus sensational extra is always sure of a considerable number of customers. The quiet-voiced and timid critic, though he possess thrice the knowledge of his brassy brother, is lost in the shuffle. Criticism, above every other craft in the modern world, save alone politics and commercial theology, is a matter of steadily loud assurance. Much of American dramatic criticism, unlike some of that in England, enjoys the steady loudness, but it lacks the necessary underlying assurance, or at least the convincing air of assurance.

In the last few years, as has been noted, we have observed the forthright endorsement, on the part of English critics, of many plays that, subsequently appraised at first hand, have given us what may delicately be described as pause. I will not pain you with a comprehensive list, but will content myself with pointing to a trio: Ronald Mackenzie's "Musical Chairs," Ronald Gow's "Gallows Glorious," and James Bridie's "The Anatomist." All — the first in particular — were announced by our trans-Atlantic confrères to be what the English fondly believe all Americans are in the habit of alluding to as the cat's whiskers. And all, upon being studied in the flesh, were seen to be the most obvious kind of dramatic mummery. Here, once again, let it be noted that the matter is not a mere case of difference of opinion. There could or can be no difference of opinion, if the opinion is grounded in any way upon rational dramatic criticism. There may be a difference of opinion founded upon difference in taste, difference in personal prejudice, or difference in experience, but not upon intrinsic dramatic merit. One and one make two in sound dramatic criticism no less than in mathematics. And as time has gone on and as a succession of such meritless plays have been peculiarly hymned as relative trumps, it has been only natural that the old American grain of salt has come to resemble the Kalabagh.

All of which should, in the logical course of events, constitute a very tasty preamble to a review of still another highly touted English play recently disclosed to American audiences. But all of which — unfortunately for those of us who like to see their convictions and arguments come out as they wish them to — doesn't. For the play in point, Mr. J. B. Priestley's "Dangerous Corner," lovingly admired by the English critics, turns out to be exactly what they said it was: a well-written, intelligent, discerning and sometimes even piercing study of human motive, impulse, conduct and reflection. Its basic fabric, true enough, is — as with most plays — woven out of one of the familiar platitudes, in this case, the disturbing consequences of truth-telling. In addition, the author has tagged a suspiciously box-office happy ending onto the tail of his play. But out of the aforesaid platitude, out even of his superficially happy coda, he has fashioned a curiously provocative and oddly insinuating slice of drama. Each turn of

[143]

character, each motivating thought, and each deduction from thought and act is logical, shrewdly understanding, and convincing.

I note various objections to the play on the part of some of its local critics. One is to the effect that it is, so the objection goes, " talky," that it substitutes words for what is called action. But it seems to me that in Priestley's words there is infinitely more dramatic action than in much of the physical movement we see on the current stage. The idea that there cannot be action — and very definite, concrete action — in words is part and parcel of the equipment of amateur dramatic criticism. Which, for example, has more quivering dramatic and theatrical movement: the single wordy lament of the mother in " Riders to the Sea " or the whole of the melodramatic " The Silver King," Caesar's soliloquy before the Sphinx in Shaw's " Caesar and Cleopatra " or the physical movement in other parts of the same play, the speeches of Synge's Christy or his acts, the loquacity of Chekhov's Constantine or the dramatic maneuvering of the other characters? Fine drama is born, first and last, of words, true words, vital and burning words, beautiful words. And there cannot be too many of them. Claptrap is the child of characters whose articulateness reposes chiefly in their legs and fists. The great dramatist is, above everything else, an eloquent talker. The hack is one who believes that human beings are only interesting and exciting when they aren't sitting quietly in a chair. (Hence, the moving pictures.)

Another observed criticism of Mr. Priestley's play as drama is that — I quote — "it insists upon talking about things that never take place upon the stage" and that, furthermore, "its dominating character is kept in the wings and is never seen by the audience." The very adjective "dominating," employed by the objecting critic, provides him with his own answer. If a playwright can keep a character off stage and yet have him dominate the play and the action, he assuredly is not open to criticism. He has set himself a feat and he has negotiated it. His play may not be a good play, but the mere fact that the audience is not permitted to see his "dominating" character does not necessarily lessen the audience's interest. The fact that the audience does not see the dominating character (Napoleon) in "The Duchess of Elba," or the dominating character (Lambertier) in Jean-Jacques Bernard's "Monsieur Lambertier," or the dominating woman character in Susan Glaspell's "Bernice," or the dominating character (Christ) in "Ben Hur" — to cite but a few examples that occur to the immediate memory — surely hasn't diminished any audience member's interest in those plays. And the same thing holds true of certain unseen dominating figures in such plays as Maeterlinck's "Intruder," Dunsany's "Gods of the Mountain," etc.

But let us look into the complaints a bit further. To argue that a play insists upon talking about things that never take place upon the stage is not to argue satisfactorily that the play is therefore deficient as theatrical drama.

Shaw's celebrated criticism of Sardou that he was in the habit of keeping his action carefully off stage and merely having it announced by letters and telegrams could not, for all its truth, persuade tens of thousands of theatregoers all over the world that Sardou's plays weren't literally bursting with theatrical drama. Sardou, true enough, was merely a very proficient hack and so perhaps is not the choicest specimen to haul into the present question. But there have been any number of superior playwrights who have equally insisted upon talking about things that never take place upon the stage and who have contrived some very good plays none the less. Shaw himself, while he cleverly pretends to be talking about things that take place upon the stage and shrewdly tricks his audiences and critics into believing it, more often actually talks about things that are taking place only — and a considerable distance away — in Downing Street, the Houses of Parliament, the Fabian Society's meeting hall, and the notebooks of Samuel Butler. Ibsen in " Little Eyolf," Echegaray in " The Great Galeoto," and — peculiarly relevant to the present critical comparison — Hervieu in " The Enigma " all talk more or less about things that do not take place upon the stage and nevertheless come off satisfactorily enough. I do not, plainly, mean to imply that Mr. Priestley is in any such select company, as yet, but at any rate he isn't, as his objecting critics mean to imply in turn, in the company of the Vicki Baums and others such whose plays, like the strippers in the burlesque halls, think that, to hold an audience, they have to show the audience everything up to and including the fig-leaf.

∽ ∽

Mr. Coward. — One is constantly reading and hearing of Mr. Noël Coward's wit. One has been reading and hearing of Mr. Noël Coward's wit for some years, ever since, in point of fact, his first comedy was uncovered to the British and American ear. And one has been reading of it, in the reviewing columns, and hearing of it, by word of audience mouth, three fold since his recent comedy, " Design For Living," has been made manifest. This enthusiastically applauded wit, it saddens me to report, I cannot for some reason or other, despite painstaking hospitality, discover. I can discover, with no effort at all, several amusing little wheezes, but all that I am able to engage in the way of the higher jocosity called wit is a suave prestidigitation of what is really nothing more than commonplace vaudeville humor. This vaudeville humor Mr. Coward cleverly brings the less humorously penetrating to accept as wit by removing its baggy pants and red undershirt and dressing it up in drawing-room style. But it remains vaudeville humor just the same.

I take the liberty to offer, seriatim, a number of examples from this " Design For Living ":

No. 1: GILDA: " You've called me a jaguar and an ox within the last two minutes. I wish you wouldn't be quite so zoölogical." (In the old small-time vaudeville halls, it ran as follows: "So I'm a goat and a jackass, huh? You talk like you was in a zoo!")

No. 2: GILDA: "Don't take off your coat and hat." OTTO: "Very well, darling, I won't, I promise you. As a matter of fact, I said to myself only this morning, 'Otto,' I said, 'Otto, you must never, never be parted from your coat and hat!'" (The old vaudeville dialogue went thus: WOMAN (*sarcastically*): "You ain't going, are you?" MAN: "No, darling, I ain't. As a matter of fact, I says to myself only this morning, 'Oswald,' I says, 'Oswald, you must never disappoint a lady. When she says "you ain't going," you ain't going!'")

No. 3: GILDA: "They call the Mauretania 'the Greyhound of the Ocean.' I wonder why?" LEO: "Because it's too long and too thin and leaps up and down." (Chronicle of obvious vaudeville genealogy unnecessary.)

No. 4: (*The telephone rings.*) LEO: "Damn!" GILDA: "Oh, Death, where is thy sting-a-ling-a-ling." (One recognizes immediately an old favorite in the Orpheum Circuit sketches.)

No. 5: GILDA: "I never said she wasn't intelligent, and I'm sure she's excellent company. She has to be. It's her job!" (Fanchon and Marco version: "That baby is good company, all right! In fact, she's so good she's incorporated!")

No. 6: LEO (*at telephone*): ". . . Of course, I'd love to. Black tie or white tie? No tie at all? That'll be much more comfortable!" (Old Keith-Albee version: "I'd like

to come, but I ain't got a thing to wear. Come anyway?
Fine! That'll be much more comfortable.")

At this point, the reader may conceivably imagine
that — following the habit of critics who are intent upon
proving a point — I have studiously combed the text of
the play for a few particularly poor specimens and have
deliberately overlooked and shrewdly concealed the more
luscious. To dispel any such belief, let us proceed.

No. 7: BIRBECK: "Do you believe the talkies will kill
the theatre?" LEO: "No, I think they'll kill the talkies."
(Who doesn't recall Tony Pastor's "So the bicycle has
hurt the theatre, has it?" "Well, not so much as it's hurt
the bicycle rider.")

No. 8: BIRBECK: "What are your ideas on marriage?"
LEO: "Garbled." (Old Poli version: "How do you stand
on marriage?" "Straddled.")

No. 9: GILDA: "That was Miss Hodge. She's had two
husbands." OTTO: "I once met a woman who'd had four
husbands." (Too sour even for vaudeville.)

No. 10: OTTO: "Why do you say that?" GILDA: "I
don't know. It came up suddenly, like a hiccup." (Vaudeville version: "What did you say?" "I didn't say nothing; that was just a belch.")

No. 11: OTTO: "What delicious-looking ham! Where
did you get it?" GILDA: "I have it specially sent from
Scotland." OTTO: "Why Scotland?" GILDA: "It lives
there when it's alive." (I quote from my records of a vaudeville act at the Palace in 1918: MAN: "These are swell

frankfurters! Where did you get 'em?" WOMAN: "From Madison Square Garden." MAN: "Why Madison Square Garden?" WOMAN: "That's where they lived when they were alive.")

No. 12: OTTO (*reproachfully*): "I don't paint their faces, Gilda. Fourth dimensional, that's what I am. I paint their souls." GILDA: "You'd have to be eighth dimensional and clairvoyant to find them." (Does one have to search one's vaudeville memory laboriously for "So you painted her soul, did you, you mug? Well, you musta been a detective to find it!")

Still a bit skeptical? Let's go on.

No. 13: GILDA: "I'm always gay on Sundays. There's something intoxicating about Sunday in London." (Pantages 1899 edition: "I'm always jolly on Sundays. There's something about Philadelphia on Sunday that gets me!")

No. 14: OTTO: "Let's have some more brandy." LEO: "That would be completely idiotic." OTTO: "Let's be completely idiotic!" (Sam, Kitty and Clara Louise Morton version: "Let's have another drink." "That'd be foolish." "But who wants to be sensible?")

No. 15: LEO (*drinking*): "Very insipid." OTTO: "Tastes like brown paper." LEO: "I've never tasted brown paper." (From the Watson, Bickel and Wrothe act (1897 A.D.): "This here drink tastes like butcher paper." "I neffer haf tasted butcher paper.")

No. 16: GRACE (*shaking hands with Otto and Leo*

[150]

who are both in evening clothes): " Oh — how do you do." Leo: " You must forgive our clothes but we've only just come off a freight boat." (From the Billy Watson Beef Trust show (*circa* 1907): Low comedian in sleeveless undershirt and tattered pants: " Don't pay no attention to my clothes, lady; I just come off the train from Newport.")

Let us now turn to the inner machinery of Mr. Coward's " wit." This machinery whirrs entirely, we find, around the stalest and most routinized of humorous devices. Device No. 1, a favorite of Mr. Coward's, is a character's repetition in a later act, for comic effect, of a line spoken seriously by another character in the earlier stages of the play. Device No. 2, believe it or not, is the periodic use of the " go to hell " line. Device No. 3 is the serio-comic promulgation of specious sentimental eloquence. I quote an example: " There's something strangely and deeply moving about young love, Mr. and Mrs. Carver. . . . Youth at the helm! . . . Guiding the little fragile barque of happiness down the river of life. Unthinking, unknowing, unaware of the perils that lie in wait for you, the sudden tempests, the sharp, jagged rocks beneath the surface. Are you never afraid? " Device No. 4 is the employment of a word or name possessed of an intrinsically comical sound. For example, Chuquicamata. And Device No. 5 is — also believe it or not — the causing of a character, who in a high pitch of indignation sweeps out of the room, to fall over something. (Sample stage direction: *"He stamps out of the room, quite beside himself with fury; on his way into the hall he falls over the package of canvases."* Whereat the characters on the stage *"break down utterly and roar with laughter."*)

Now for the original and profound philosophy underlying Mr. Coward's great wit. I exhibit samples:

No. 1: GILDA: "Why don't I marry Otto?" ERNEST: "Yes. Is there a real reason, or just a lot of faintly affected theories?" GILDA: "There's a very real reason." ERNEST: "Well?" GILDA: "I love him."

No. 2: LEO: "I'm far too much of an artist to be taken in by the old cliché of shutting out the world and living for my art alone. There's just as much bunk in that as there is in a cocktail party at the Ritz."

No. 3: LEO: "I'm dreadfully suspicious of people liking things too much — things that matter, I mean. There's too much enthusiasm for Art going on nowadays. It smears out the high-lights."

No. 4: GILDA: "Do you know a lot about ships now?" OTTO: "Not a thing. The whole business still puzzles me dreadfully. I know about starboard and port, of course, and all the different bells; but no one has yet been able to explain to me satisfactorily why, the first moment a rough sea occurs, the whole thing doesn't turn upside down!"

No. 5: GILDA: "I think I want to cry again." OTTO: "There's nothing like a good cry."

No. 6: OTTO: "Have I changed so dreadfully?"
GILDA: "It isn't you that's changed—it's time and experience and new circumstances!"

No. 7: Gilda and Otto have been discussing what Mr. Coward alludes to as "love among the artists." OTTO: "But we should have principles to hang on to, you know. This floating about without principles is so very dangerous." GILDA: "Life is for living!"

No. 8: LEO: "Science is our only hope, the only hope for humanity! We've wallowed in false mysticism for centuries; we've fought and suffered and died for foolish beliefs, which science has proved to be as ephemeral as smoke. Now is the moment to open our eyes fearlessly and look at the truth!"

No. 9: GILDA: "The human race is a let-down, a bad, bad let-down! I'm disgusted with it. It thinks it's progressed but it hasn't; it thinks it's risen above the primeval slime but it hasn't—it's still wallowing in it! It's still clinging to us, clinging to our hair and our eyes and our souls. We've invented a few small things that make noises, but we haven't invented one big thing that creates quiet, endless peaceful quiet . . . something to deaden the sound of our emotional yellings and screechings and suffocate our psychological confusions." (Ah there, Shaw, Priestley and Co.!)

We now pass to a consideration of the freshness of Mr. Coward's broader humors. Herewith, specimens:

No. 1: LEO: "I remember a friend of mine called Mrs.

Purdy being very upset once when her house in Dorset fell into the sea." GRACE: "How terrible!" LEO: "Fortunately, Mr. Purdy happened to be in it at the time."

No. 2: GILDA: "It's very hot today, isn't it?" ERNEST: "Why not open the window?" GILDA: "I never thought of it."

No. 3: GILDA: "We must get it straight, somehow." LEO: "Yes, we must get it straight and tie it up with ribbons with a bow on the top. Pity it isn't Valentine's Day!"

No. 4: LEO: "Doesn't the Eye of Heaven mean anything to you?" GILDA: "Only when it winks!"

No. 5: GILDA: "Think if television came in suddenly, and everyone who rang up was faced with Miss Hodge!" (*Miss Hodge enters. She is dusty and extremely untidy.*)

No. 6: OTTO (*at telephone*): "Dinner on the seventh? Yes, I should love to. You don't mind if I come as Marie Antoinette, do you? (*Pause*) I have to go to a fancy dress ball."

Mr. Coward's " daring sophistication " is still another enchantment of his public and his critics. Let us, in turn, consider this daring sophistication in the light of its most trenchant specimen lines:

No. 1: GILDA: "After all, it (the London *Times*) is the organ of the nation." LEO: "That sounds vaguely pornographic to me." (Regards to Mae West.)

No. 2: GILDA: "The honeymoon would be thrilling, wouldn't it? Just you and me, alone, finding out about each other." LEO: "I'd be very gentle with you, very ten-

der." GILDA: " You'd get a sock in the jaw, if you were! "
(Regards to Michael Arlen.)

No. 3: GILDA: " Tell me, Mr. Mercuré, what do you
think of the modern girl? " LEO: " A silly bitch." (Regards to Elmer Harris.)

No. 4: OTTO: " Are you trying to lure me to your
wanton bed? " GILDA: " What would you do if I did? "
OTTO: " Probably enjoy it very much." (Regards to Va-
leska Suratt, Paul Potter and " The Girl With the Whooping Cough," 1908 A.D.)

In order to deceive his audiences and critics into believing that all this vaudeville-hall humor and juvenile
naughtiness is excessively recherché stuff, it is Mr. Coward's practice, as I have hinted, to have it spoken by actors in evening dress and to intersperse it liberally with
worldly allusions to the more fashionable restaurants, ho-
tels, yachts, duchesses' houses and watering places. When
Mr. Coward is not alluding condescendingly to something
like the Duke of Westminster's yacht, one may be sure
that he is either alluding affectionately to the Carlton Hotel or commenting somewhat superciliously on the marble
bathrooms at the George V. His plays are also usually rich
in references to the bigger ocean liners, modern French
painters, various opera composers, the better sherries and
brandies, Claridge's, fashionable London churches, valets
— always " in white coats " — butlers, footmen, upper
housemaids, secretaries, the Ritz, smart house parties in
Hampshire, backgammon, squash courts, terraces " with

striped awnings," some casino or other, and the more expensive makes of automobiles. And, naturally, to emphasize the magnificent modishness of it all, Mr. Coward is careful to derogate at due intervals such bourgeois institutions as world cruises, newspapers, households that can afford but one maid, and the music of Richard Wagner.

In order to establish beyond all audience doubt the perfect equilibrium of his sophistication and to persuade it that he is superior even to his own highest flights of philosophical reasoning, it is Mr. Coward's habit to disgorge the philosophical pearls reposing in his mind and then to bring another character to offer a facetious remark about, or to chuckle derisively over, each of the aforesaid pearls. Either that or, by way of passing himself off for a magnanimous intellect, to place his most serious convictions in the mouth of a character who is slightly intoxicated. Thus, let one character speak Mr. Coward's mind about some cynical aspect of civilization, and another like clock-work is ready with some such retort as "That is definitely macabre!" Thus, let a character express a sentiment of some delicacy and another is ready with a deprecation of him as a rank sentimentalist. Thus, let the action turn to normal drama and a character is ready with the mocking exclamation, "Bravo, Deathless Drama!" Thus, let Mr. Coward venture what he considers in his heart to be a first-rate and saucy bit of humor and another character is ready with "That was a cheap gibe!" And thus, let a character express Mr. Coward's sober convictions as to Life and another is in the offing duly to jump in at the conclusion with a facetious " Laife, that's what it is, just laife." And so it goes — always the pseudo-philosopher and commentator taking what he writes with perfect gravity and surrounding himself, fearful and feeling the need of ideational protection, with a procession of minstrel end-men to hop up after each observation and minimize it with a joke.

Mr. Coward occupies the successful place in our theatre today that the late Clyde Fitch occupied twenty and thirty years ago. Both are of a playwriting piece, though Mr. Coward has not yet contrived anything nearly so good as Fitch's " The Truth." And both have been overpraised and overestimated ridiculously. Where are the plays of Fitch now? Where will the plays of Mr. Coward be when as many years have passed? As in the case of my critical reflections on Fitch in his fashionable heyday, I leave the answer to the calendar.

As to " Design For Living " specifically — it has been greeted by the reviewers as something very remarkable — I can see in it little more than a pansy paraphrase of " Candida," theatrically sensationalized with " daring," gay allusions to hermaphrodites, " gipsy queens," men dressed as women, etc., and with various due references to " predatory feminine carcasses " and to women as bitches. The big scene is simply a rehash of the one played by the

two drunken women in the same author's "Fallen Angels" and here given, relevantly, into the hands of two
men.

ŝ   ŝ

Mr. Kaufman. — Finding Mr. George S. Kaufman's name
attached to "Dinner at Eight" comes with something of
the same surprise that would be associated, in an opposite
direction, with finding the Rev. Dr. Clarence True Wilson's name attached to a bottle of good beer. This Kaufman is one of the higher grade men involved in the American drama; he stands for something much better than the
general run of his contemporaries; he has a wit and a viewpoint, an originality and a resolution, superior to three-
quarters of them. And what do we lately discover him at?
We discover him, not without a bit of critical gooseflesh,
collaborating with Miss Edna Ferber on a pail of deliber-
ate box-office and Hollywood bait, modelled imitatively
after "Grand Hotel," that might pass muster with a much
lesser man, but that, coming from him, causes one critic
who respects him to confer upon him, with appropriate
ceremonies, the *Croix de Fromage.*

The great commercial success of the Vicki Baum play,
together with the success of the mooing picture made from
it, has resulted in many transcriptions on the part of persons eager to horn in on some of the ready-made pelf.
What Frau Baum did for the hotel, a swarm of copycats
in the theatre, in the films, and in fiction, have attempted

to duplicate in the case of the office building (" Skyscraper Souls "), the ocean liner (" Transatlantic "), and almost every other species of man-made structure save only — thus far — that celebrated by Mr. Chic Sale. Everybody, in short, has been rewriting " Grand Hotel " and now Mr. Kaufman and Miss Ferber get into line with a paraphrase concerned with the events surrounding the institution known as a formal dinner party. Instead of the lobby, the bar, the corridors and the rooms of the hotel, with the threads of the lives of the persons in them woven into a tangled skein, we have the hostess' boudoir, the servants' quarters, the houses and offices of the bidden guests, the dining-room, etc., with the threads of the lives of the characters in them similarly gathered into such a skein.

Nor does what has come recently to be a rubber-stamp stop here. Among the characters are such stock figures as the fluttery, middle-aged, snobbish and vulgar hostess, avid of social favor, out of the early Tarkington-Wilson drama, the passée stage beauty who indulges in reminiscence of old Delmonico's and the days when swains thronged at the stage door, the harassed man of affairs who (actually) clutches at his breast periodically, indicating that he is doomed to die of a heart attack, the faded male movie idol pathetically trying to pretend to himself and to others that he is still being sought after, the blustering Western business man, the married worm who finds his only pleasure and romance in sneaking off to the movies, the hard-boiled hotel bellboy intent upon getting his tips, the brash Broadway Jewish booking agent, and so on.

While here and there in the manuscript one encounters some moments of lively and authentic Kaufman humor — he is a writer who couldn't be completely humorless if he tried — the bulk of that script reveals little that has come to be expected from his pen. Indeed, even some of the more humorous lines such, for example, as the reference to the inordinate and puzzling activity of fire engines as soon as night falls, hark back more or less familiarly to the early Margaret Mayo farces. And such dramatic lines as " Get out before I kick you out! ", such dramatic devices as the blackmailing maid-servant who picks up her philandering mistress' valuable ring, tries it on her finger and suggestively remarks to her mistress that it looks well there, such bits of business as a flighty woman's flurry to get into a seductive negligée against the arrival of the good-looking young doctor, such other bits as the aforesaid vacuous woman's hasty seizure of a profound book and her pretense of being immersed in it upon the announcement of a caller, such Baumish wham as the wholesale tragedy and woe that descend upon the characters whose life threads are caught up by the innocent dinner party: the host's loss of his fortune and his imminent death from worry and heart strain, the cheap seduction of the host's daughter, the suicide of one guest, the betrayal of another by his wife, the murderous attempt of one servant upon another's life, etc. — such items in combination are hard to reconcile with Mr. Kaufman's past performances and reputation.

" But anyway," argue Mr. Kaufman and Miss Ferber in theatrical parlance, " whatever you say against it, you must admit that it plays! "

The same answer might be made in behalf of a second-hand tin piano.

∽ ∽

Mr. Hecht. — Among the men writing for the American theatre, Mr. Ben Hecht is one of the most sharply ironical and bitingly honest. As in Mr. Kaufman's case, it also comes as a surprise, therefore, to find his name combined with that of a gentleman named Fowler on the exhibit called " The Great Magoo." That is, it comes as a surprise unless one recalls that Mr. Hecht has lately been in literary contact with Hollywood and unless one recalls, further, that the newspapers not so long ago noted that he had been commissioned to do a scenario suitable to the talents of Mr. James Cagney. That " The Great Magoo," accordingly, was written less for the stage than for the subsequent screen is more or less apparent.

The play, as shown on the stage, is exactly the soufflée of smut and sentimentality that is so close to the movie impresarios' hearts. It combines, in alternating doses, assaults upon the humor of such persons as are wont to go into paroxysms of ribald laughter at the public mention of a water-closet and upon the somewhat tenderer sensibilities of such — they are usually one and the same — as experience an inner fluttering at the spectacle of a baffled and noble love at length coming into its own. At bottom, the theme is one which, if he encountered it in anyone's else play, would cause Hecht to let out a yell of derision that would blast all the stone quarries in his native Nyack, to wit, the theme of the harlot redeemed by Pure Love. Laying hold of the ancient claptrap — and with what seems to be a straight face, as the writing of the sentimental passages is the best in the play — Hecht and his partner have sought to conceal their boyish shame by obstreperously embellishing its outer fringe with words, phrases and bits of business that would drive Lady Chatterley's lover right into the arms of Jane Austen. This embellishment has an air of unmistakable insincerity and dishonesty. It suggests the loud self-incriminations as to his own canine genealogy on the part of a man who has hit his thumb with a hammer. It has all the ring of the monosyllabic snort of an abashed little boy who has been surprised by his comrades in the act of kissing the schoolteacher. It is, in short, jingo. Well, not all of it, for there is one scene into which it fits properly and honestly — a scene wherein the miscellaneously constituted young wife of a champion flag-pole-sitter entertains, with some difficulty, a midnight caller while her husband spies upon her bedchamber from his somewhat distant perch with a pair of powerful binoculars. This is good low comedy and the

[162]

manner of its expression is legitimate. But the rest is merely college-boy washroom stuff.

And what is more, it is sadly out-dated. Listening to the Hecht-Fowler lower vocabulary takes one back to the theatre of a half dozen years or more ago, when a multitude of young men, bursting with gleeful shouts the restraining chains of the earlier stage, let go nightly with such a torrent of deity-damning, mother-derogating, sex-celebrating *mots* that, when eleven o'clock came around, the auditor didn't know whether to reach under the chair for his hat or under the bar for the bar-towel. The drama has changed a lot since then. And the Messrs. Hecht and Fowler, though they may not realize it, today look dramatically very much like sailors with their hands on their hips.

ᔑ ᔑ

Mr. Rice. — A trip to Russia, so far as writers are concerned, seems to have the same disastrous consequences as a trip to Hollywood. Let the average writer spend so little as two or three days hanging around Moscow eating herring soup and, when he recrosses the border, he is a Changed Man. The mere sight of an automobile that costs more than $200 makes him froth indignantly at the mouth, and the spectacle of people who have had enough to eat induces in him so great a disgust that it takes him a full year to recover. I know one young writer, a graduate of Harvard who used to have his silk socks made especially to order, who spent five days in Moscow and who the next week was locked up in a French hoosegow for walloping a waiter in one of the Paris boulevard cafés because the latter had the audacity to suggest to him a crêpe Suzette.

As Hollywood can take a hitherto competent writer and send him back to civilization indistinguishable from a contributor to *Common Sense,* so Russia can take one with a hitherto well-poised and competent mind and send him back a loon. Any number of previously canny and astute writers have gone into Russia with calm intelligence and have come out a short time later acting and writing as if they had guzzled six kegs of vodka. However much they may have with an affectionate satisfaction viewed money when they went in, they reappear with the conviction that the possession of anything over fifty-two cents is excessively odious. And the same reverse English obtains in the case of most of their other former tastes and prejudices.

Mr. Elmer Rice appears to be still another gentleman of the pen who has had things happen to his psyche after a short trip to Russia. True enough, a little of the toxic quality was discernible in him even before he stopped eating good food for a couple of weeks and pleasurably freezing his dactyls off in the interests of the Higher Ideal, but he now reveals himself to have gone the whole hog. Mr. Rice has done some very good work for the American stage. It is accordingly something of a pity to observe him thus flying off the handle and turning out this depressing propaganda stuff. His three latest plays amount to little more than dramatized *New Masses* editorials.

∽ ∽

Mr. Wallace. — There are just two reasons, or justifications, for a writing man doing a prodigious amount of work. One is to achieve something eventually beautiful and, with it, a deserved glory. The other is to make a pot of money. If a man doesn't achieve one or the other, his life may be put down — by himself as well as by others — as a failure.

The late Edgar Wallace did an enormous amount of work, producing plays, novels, short stories and what not by the train-load. Much of this work was popular, but none of it had the slightest artistic reason for being. What is more, according to the published reports of his estate after his recent death, it made him, considering its bulk, only a fairish amount of money. Hence, in the way the world looks at such things — and looks at it soundly — he was a dud. True enough, he was, as has been noted, popular, which is to say that thousands of inferior persons admired what he wrote. But no man worth his salt, even in his own secret estimation, takes pride in any such jitney *ḳudos*. It is, indeed, down in his better and more ambitious heart, just a little disgusting to him. True enough, again, Wallace liked the superficial luxuries of life and his income, while it lasted, was sufficient to allow him to gratify his tastes in that direction. But the gratification of such tastes is a transient thing, as even the fellow of most gala impulses only too well knows, and is a sorry makeshift and but a momentary opiate for wishes closer and deeper and infinitely more thrilling.

There are dolts who imagine that hard work is its own reward and these will accordingly say that Wallace doubtless got a sufficient excitement out of it, whatever else it may or may not subsequently have brought him. But hard work is exciting only if it is followed by a worthy recompense of one kind or another: fame founded upon the quality of what one has done, or fortune, or, at least, personal satisfaction grounded upon the firm conviction that what one has written is grand stuff. As I have said, Wallace did not win such fame; he did not win such fortune; and I doubt if, in his innards, he ever for a moment believed that his work touched even remotely the borders of quality. He was a "successful" writer in a relative sense — he didn't make one-tenth the money that such a ten-thousand times superior writer as Shaw, say, has made — and he gained only a tawdry renown. His career should be an inspiration, in an opposite direction, to all young and aspiring writers.

∽ ∽

Mr. Lawson. — I observe that certain of the appraisers of Mr. John Howard Lawson's dramatic efforts, while finding fault with other phases of his plays, nevertheless proclaim him a fellow of considerable cerebral puissance. His plays may not be all that they should be, say these gentlemen in effect, but one can still detect in them a mind much above the general, and one inhabited by rich and fruity thoughts. Just how these assayers of mental profundity arrive at their conclusion is something of a puzzle, for all that most of the rest of us are able to discern in Mr. Lawson is an intellectual content which, measured in terms of alcoholic volume, hardly exceeds that of prohibition Anheuser-Busch.

There is, of course, no reason why it should be demanded or desired of Mr. Lawson — or of any other playwright, for that matter — that he be a mastermind. The writing of sound drama does not impose upon a playwright the obligation of an herculean intellect. The prescription to the contrary is the symptom of youthful criticism that seeks to hide its own complete hollow-headedness in an indignant invocation of mental gifts in others. But that is not the point. The point, rather, is that, in the process of the invocation alluded to, the youthful hollow-headed criticism, being unable to appreciate genuine intelligence even when and should it see it, mistakes for intelligence any sufficiently impassioned and cajoling restatement of its own prejudices, however fundamentally scrimp in poise and sense. It is because Mr. Lawson engages in such restatements that the youthful criticism, along with criticism that is still going around in mental diapers for all its greater age, endorses him as a thinker.

In its giddy eagerness to hail him as a very heady fellow, the same criticism does Mr. Lawson the injustice of overlooking certain other attributes that he is not without. Among these are passion, sincerity and a degree of independence. Unfortunately, however, in conjunction with the aforesaid attributes there is no noticeable gift for dramaturgy. As a playwright, he is on the same level that he is as a philosopher, which level, it need not impolitely be reindicated, is considerably below the water-line. In none of the work that he has done for the theatre has he shown any skill at playwriting. The best that he has been able to manage has been an indifferent copy of the German Expressionism. The worst has resulted in at least four plays that are as completely bad as anything that amateur playwriting has contributed to the local stage. He remains still another example of corruption and possible ruin at the hands of criticism which, in his earlier days, foolishly praised the superficial aspects of his work — thus leading him contentedly astray — and failed to preserve him to himself by neglecting to point out to him his basic weaknesses as a playwright. The stage, after all, is above all else for playwrights. It is, only and long after that, the place for excursions into intellectual enterprise, fervor, and protest. As Mr. Lawson now stands, he amounts to very little. He does not know, apparently, the fundamentals of dramatic composition; he does not know how to elaborate character; he does not know how to achieve even his intrinsically valid effects. He is, with his heat and fire and passion, much like a great lover who hasn't got a girl.

Consider his two most recent plays: " The Pure In Heart " and " Gentlewoman." In a sententious program note, he announced that the former was " an attempt to achieve a mood quite foreign to the realistic theatre." Continuing, he announced that it was " an effort to bring a certain sort of modern poetry into the theatre . . . not the poetry of blank verse and measured sentences, (but) the turbulent crude rhythm of the dynamic world in which we live." Well, having ingested the program note, what did we see? We saw the cheap old hokum story of the poor, innocent country girl who, ambition-ridden, comes to New York and encounters all the stereotyped pitfalls — chief among them sex — until pure love and death redeem her. We saw the " mood quite foreign to the realistic theatre " achieved by having a few fiddlers play off-stage tear-music at appropriate intervals and by turning on a lavender light at such moments as O'Neill or Maxwell Anderson would raise hell if a plain, ordinary white or amber one wasn't turned on. And we heard " a certain sort of modern poetry " that sounded exactly like the dialogue in a Hollywood pent-house talkie, and saw " the turbulent crude rhythm of the dynamic world in which we live " interpreted mainly in terms of a half dozen ballet dancers and some pistol shots. In a word what we saw and heard, ladies and gentlemen, was the bunk.

In the latter play, Mr. Lawson abandoned for the moment his great experimentation, essayed to write in the more orthodox dramatic form, and proved that he was entirely as incapable in the one as in the other. His idea of lending a new vitality to the thematic corpse of the lady of high station who succumbs to the mentality and anatomical allure of a man of the people was to make his hero talk like a freshman radical and his proud lady like a Wampas Baby alumna. His idea of a novel moist dramatic situation was to bring in a loyal maid-servant and have her touchingly sob her intention of remaining with her mistress who found herself bankrupt and unable to pay further wages. His idea of a novel dramatic character was a butler who quietly allowed that he spent his spare time delving into various minor classics, and who surprised his male questioners with his philosophical acumen. His idea of humor consisted in such badinage as a remark about a lady-in-waiting and the query as to what she was waiting for. And his idea of fresh and piquant simile and metaphor took the form of allusions to " the eye of a dead codfish " and " the sex life of a clam."

Mr. Lawson, in short, is a very ambitious, if defectively equipped, playwright who has spent his dramatic life vacillating between Greenwich Village and Hollywood and who has not been able to graduate from either. His plays, as a consequence, are ridiculously fuddled and amateurish mixtures of Greenwich Village sex and Cherry Lane experimentation on the one hand and of Hollywood theme song and Metro-Goldwyn lot fancy on the other.

ᔡ ᔡ

Miss Stein. — By way of a final guzzle and a good critical song ringing clear, let us put Gertrude Stein on the table and determine, now that her self-admitted *chef d'œuvre,* " Four Saints in Three Acts," has been delivered to us, just what — as in Mr. Lawson's case — is her artistic alcoholic content.

It is Miss Stein's stout argument that the meaning and sense of words placed together is of no importance; that it is only their sound and rhythm that count. This, in certain specific phases of artistic enterprise, may — for all one's initial impulse to impolite titter — be not entirely so silly as it sounds. Beautiful music often is meaningless (in the same sense of the word) and yet finds its effect and importance in sound and rhythm. Poetry, also, often finds its true reason and being in a complete lack of intelligence and in the vapors of lovely sound and lulling rhythms. Painting, too, need not have " meaning," nor " sense," but may project its power alone by form (which is rhythm) and by color (which is the equivalent of sound). Even drama itself may have little meaning and sense, yet may evoke a curious meaning-within-absence-of-meaning (regards to Dreiser) none the less; for example, Strindberg's " Spook Sonata " or — to go to extremes in even absurdity — something like Mr. Lawson's " The International."

Up to this point, there conceivably may be something

in Miss Stein's literary bolshevism. But now let us see how she combines theory with practice. In demonstration and proof of her conviction that the meaning and sense of words are of infinitely less significance than their sound and rhythm she presents to us, in the *chef d'œuvre* mentioned, such verbal matrimony as the following (I mercifully quote but three samples):

1. "To know to know to love her so. Four saints prepare for saints. It makes it well fish. Four saints it makes it well fish."

2. "Might have as would be as would be as within nearly as out. It is very close close and closed. Closed closed to let letting closed close close close close in justice in join in joining. This is where to be at at water at snow snow show show one one sun and sun snow show and no water no water unless unless why unless. Why unless why unless they were loaning it here loaning intentionally. Believe two three. What could be sad beside beside very attentively intentionally and bright."

3. "The difference between saints forget-me-nots and mountains have to have to have to at a time."

Repressing a horse-laugh and hitching up our earmuffs, let us meditate this arch-delicatessen. That Miss Stein is absolutely correct in announcing that it has not either meaning or sense, I hope no one will be so discourteous as to dispute. But if Miss Stein argues that, on the other hand and to its greater virtue, it has rhythm and beautiful sound, I fear that I, for one, will have to constitute myself a cad and a bounder and inform her that she is fish and it does not make it well fish either. In point of fact, anyone with half an ear to rhythm and sound (whether in song, in reading, or in recitation) can tell her that any such arrangement of words — to pick at random — as " beside beside very attentively intentionally and bright " is not only lacking in rhythm and pleasant sound but that, in addition, it is painfully cacophonous. It is perfectly true that words shrewdly strung together may be meaningless and may still sound better than words strung together with some meaning — take Edgar Guest's poetry, for instance — but one fears that Miss Stein has not mastered the trick which she so enthusiastically sponsors and advocates. I am no Gertrude Stein, but I venture constructively to offer her a laboratory specimen of what she is driving at and fails to achieve. The example: " Sell a cellar, door a cellar, sell a cellar cellar-door, door adore, adore a door, selling cellar, door a cellar, cellar cellar-door." There is damned little meaning and less sense in such a sentence, but there is, unless my tonal balance is askew, twice more rhythm and twice more lovely sound in it than in anything, equally idiotic, that Miss Gertrude ever confected.

The contention of a number of music critics who have reviewed Miss Stein's opera is that, inasmuch as one can catch very few of the words in the average opera and, not being bi-lingual, would understand most of them not at all even if one did catch them, it is of no consequence that

Miss Stein's lyrics are completely meaningless and absurd. If both Miss Stein and her sympathetic critics are right — that is, if sense does not figure in the matter, if the rhythm and sound are all that count, and if in opera one can, anyway, only at very rare intervals decipher the words that are being sung — may it not be suggested that Miss Stein abandon in her future operas all such hash as she writes — which unnecessarily irritates the intelligent and the judicious — and achieve a sound name and operatic position for herself by substituting for it such simple and beautifully rhythmical sequences as eenie, meenie, minie, mo, or the even more simple and effective do, re, mi, fa, so, la, si, do? Miss Stein, further, is not sincere. Though she professes to be the arch-enemy of the apostles of meaning in the written word, she every now and again halts abruptly in the midst of her verbal monkeyshines and writes some such grammatically orthodox, clear and simple sentence as, " If it were possible to kill five thousand Chinamen by pressing a button, would it be done? " One begins to believe that Gertie is a very shrewd and sapient girl who deliberately plans her writing performances as absurdity and who appreciates that if you keep up absurdity long enough, and with a perfectly straight face, there will always be critics who will mistake the *tour de force* for some strange and inscrutable kind of wayward genius.

One more point and we conclude our performance. Granting for the moment Miss Stein her premise that the rhythm and sound of words are more important than their sense and meaning, may we ask her how she feels about a possibly perfect combination of the two? Does she, or does she not, believe that beautiful rhythm and beautiful sound combined with sense and meaning may constitute something finer than mere rhythm and sound wedded to meaninglessness and lack of sense? While she is pardonably hesitating to make up her mind, let us ask her to consider such things, for example, as the hauntingly beautiful Marlowe speech in Conrad's "Youth," or Caesar's parting from Cleopatra in the Shaw play, or Dubedat's from his wife in the same writer's "The Doctor's Dilemma," or Brassbound's from Cicely in the same writer's "Captain Brassbound's Conversion," or Candida's from the poet Eugene in the same writer's "Candida," or Galsworthy's "To say goodbye! To her and Youth and Passion! To the only salve for the aching that Spring and Beauty bring — the aching for the wild, the passionate, the new, that never quite dies in a man's heart. Ah, well, sooner or later all men had to say goodbye to that. All men — all men! . . . He crouched down before the hearth. There was no warmth in that fast-blackening ember, but it still glowed like a dark-red flower. And while it lived he crouched there, as though it were that to which he was saying goodbye. And on the door he heard the girl's ghostly knocking. And beside him — a ghost among the ghostly presences — she stood. Slowly the glow blackened, till the last spark had died out." Or a hundred passages from Shakespeare, or a score from George Moore. Or some of the prose of

Max Beerbohm, or Cabell's Jurgen chapter, "The Dorothy Who Did Not Understand," or Maurya's wail to the sea in the Synge play, or some such line from Sean O'Casey's "Within the Gates" as "To sing our song with the song that is sung by a thousand stars of the evening," or Dunsany's little two hundred word fable, "The Assignation," from its beginning "Fame singing in the highways, and trifling as she sang, with sordid adventurers, passed the poet by" to her final whisper "I will meet you in the graveyard at the back of the Workhouse in a hundred years."

Come, Gertie, let us hear what you have to say. Meanwhile, one fears that one will have to regard you as the Helen Kane, the Boop-a-doop girl, of modern literature.

CHAPTER XII

Producers and Productions

∽ ∽

Mr. Hopkins. — Wherever persons interested in the theatre have been gathered together during the last four or five years, one has heard the same husky whisper: " What in the world is it that has happened to Arthur Hopkins? " The question, in view of Mr. Hopkins' proud position in the theatre antecedently, together with his quondam admirable experimentation, skilful direction and shrewd sense of manuscript values, has been an understandable one. For it is something of a theatrical phenomenon that one like him should so suddenly, in all the particulars named, not only go to pot, but go to pot in so peculiarly unfathomable a manner. The once alive exploratory impulse seems to have died; the once telling stage direction has become something almost amateurish; and the once judicious eye to manuscript merit appears to have gone totally and completely blind.

Any man who contends as I do that it is no particularly occult business to tell, from an advance reading of a dramatic manuscript, whether a play is good or bad, is, of course, often looked upon as either a bumptious boaster or a plain blockhead by persons who believe that, unlike a book in type-script, a written sheet of music, or a copy of an after-dinner speech, a play manuscript is somehow a very mysterious and enigmatically multilocular affair about which absolutely nothing can be foretold until it is shown on a stage before an audience of nitwits. That it should be, and really is, no very difficult business for an ordinarily intelligent person to judge the quality of a play (if, true enough, not always the extent of its box-office success, though almost always the extent of its certain failure) from a perusal of the mere manuscript is regarded in various theatrical quarters as quite unbelievable. Yet here we have Mr. Hopkins, who is anything but dumb, not only selecting for production in recent years scripts that have been as obviously and painfully meritless as those in his earlier producing days were laudable, but evidently full of a conviction that they would stand a chance in the theatre. That miserable judgment has alone been responsible must be taken for granted, as Mr. Hopkins — who only last season rejected Clare Kummer's (his original discovery) "Her Master's Voice" as being no good in favor of Philip Barry's "The Joyous Season" — cannot fall back on the usual apology that there wasn't anything better available. In the late years that he has been wasting himself on mediocrities, doomed to failure, there have been to my definite knowledge no less than ten or twelve immensely superior plays that he might have had, had he been able to detect their superiority. And at the very moment that he concluded to produce "The Joyous Season," that melancholy example of slipshod play-writing, there was aching to be produced the one play that in other years he would have given his very chemise to produce, to wit, the splendid and shining " Within the Gates " of Sean O'Casey, already hailed as a masterpiece, after a reading of the manuscript, by some of the most perceptive critics in England and America. Or, if he didn't want masterpieces, with their occasional box-office doubt-fulness, there were ready to his hand two or three lesser plays (also, like "The Joyous Season," with religious themes) that were relatively better on all counts than that play and that doubtless would have stood a better chance with paying audiences — Molnár's " Miracle in the Moun-tains," for example, for one.

Then, let us take the matter of production and direc-tion. We need look no farther than this " The Joyous Sea-son " to observe the deterioration of the Hopkins crafts-manship. Always given to a fondness for easy, unforced and naturalistic playing, Mr. Hopkins has in the last half dozen years carried his direction in this regard to such an extreme that the impression one gets is less of easy, un-forced and naturalistic playing than of too few rehearsals. He confounds lifelessness with ease, and tedium with casualness. It has for some time now also been evident that the fundamental trouble with the various sorely beset and deeply agitated families in the plays he produces — and in particular with the Farley family in the Barry play — is that they never sit down. Mr. Hopkins seems to imagine that a play will immediately go to pieces if one of the actors seats himself for so little as two minutes. He accordingly stands 'em up, as the phrase goes, everywhere, unfortunately, but in the audiences. That the crises of drama may not be so very dissimilar to those in life and that they more often occur in human beings' lives when the latter are either sitting — or, even more often, lying — down, he apparently declines to permit himself for a moment to believe.

His production methods and manuscript manipulation, since his lamentable decline, were brilliantly illustrated in the instance of this Barry exhibit, bad as it itself was. He took a play called, without the slightest ironic intent, " The Joyous Season " — that is, Christmas — and satisfied himself in indicating its inner mood merely by hanging a couple of holly wreaths on the windows of the house wherein the action occurred and by lighting the stage so dimly that the comedy was turned into a funeral sermon. He took an Irish family, among its number five lusty Micks, and had them all celebrate the Yuletide by serving and drinking — praise be the saints! — sherry. He so directed the mien and manner of the stage Catholics that they were indistinguishable from Methodists. He allowed his old Irish biddy at one point in the proceedings — actually! — to do an old Harrigan and Hart shuffle-dance. Having gathered together an excellent acting company, he took all the dramatic life out of it by centering his lighting at mid-stage, dimming it to the vanishing point at the left and right, and so converting the play's text into a succession of spot-light monologues and duologues, with the actors momentarily silent shunted into the darkness and practically out of the flow of the play. He further depressed what minimum of action there was by a static grouping of those characters who were not, for the moment, figuring in the dialogue, for all the world like scrubs on the sidelines waiting to be called into the game. His well-to-do Farley family evidently were in arrears on their electricity bill, for they apparently couldn't get the company to turn on the lights in the hall, which — despite the fact that the butler and maid-servant had to do all the serving through it — was so pitch dark that the latter should at least have been considerately equipped with pocket-flashes. He — but I refrain, lest continuance resolve itself into too lengthy cataloguing.

And who am I who writes thus of Mr. Hopkins? I am the critic who, years ago, wrote the preface to his book on stage direction and production and who in that preface hailed him as the most intelligent, the most discerning, and infinitely the most promising director and producer in the American theatre!

∽ ∽

Mystery Legend. — Deep in the cerebrum of most theatrical producers, however much they may deny it, is the conviction that, of all present-day forms of stage entertainment, the so-called mystery play is, when all is said and

done, the safest box-office gamble. It is for this reason that
the average fly-by-night producer, or the average regular
producer with whom things haven't been going so well,
usually seeks to make himself some easy money with one
or another such specimen of drama. Having long edified
myself with the impudent assurance that the average producer knows infinitely less about his business than the
average business man in almost any other quarter, I have
meditated his faith in the commercial value of these mystery plays, have done a little looking into my records, and
have bought myself two congratulatory drinks on my
own larger sapience. What have I found? Investigating
the statistics of the last two and one-half seasons alone,
I have found that, far from being any longer a pretty good
gamble, the mystery play seems to be one of the very
worst.

In these two and one-half seasons, out of a grand total
of twenty-two mystery plays produced — I omit " Murder
at the Vanities " as falling into the musical show category
— but a solitary one has achieved even a fair success in the
theatre, and that one, " Riddle Me This," was not, in the
strict sense of the word, a mystery play at all. " Trick For
Trick " and " Criminal At Large," two other mystery
plays, had a superficial air of success in that they were kept
running for a while, but I am given to understand that the
box-office intake on them was far from satisfactory to the
respective investors. (The sale of movie rights has nothing
to do with our immediate theme: the failure of mystery

plays at the theatre ticket-window.) Look over the list of failures: " Three Times the Hour," " Black Tower," " The House of Doom " (a honey!), " The Fatal Alibi " (despite Charles Laughton and Jed Harris direction), " Zombie," " Monkey," " The Border Land," " The Man Who Changed His Name " (for all Edgar Wallace's pull with the drugstore intellects), " Nine Pine Street " (a mystery melodramatized into fact), " Firebird " (despite an admirable Gilbert Miller production), " Ten Minute Alibi " (though it got a good boost from the press), " Keeper of the Keys," " The Dark Tower " (though written in part by the skilful George Kaufman and directed by him), " Invitation To a Murder," " The Drums Begin," " The Locked Room," " Halfway To Hell," " A Hat, A Coat, A Glove," and " Order Please."

The theory that there is a lot of money in mystery plays is like the theory — recently affectionately embraced by Eugene O'Neill in the case of " Days Without End " and by Arthur Hopkins and Philip Barry in the case of " The Joyous Season " — that Catholics will pack a theatre to the doors and turn in a gigantic profit on any play dealing sympathetically with Catholicism. Just where and how this latter theory ever dug its toes into the turf and got off to a running start is, in view of the facts, rather difficult to make out. The facts are that not one modern play dealing primarily with Catholicism has ever made a nickel in the theatre. It isn't that Catholics are so different, when it comes to theatregoing, from any other sect; it is simply that when they go to the theatre they go for diversion, like anyone else, and not for theological and ecclesiastical purposes. The three most conspicuous loyal Catholic local theatregoers in the last decade, Al Smith, Jimmy Walker and Dudley Field Malone, might always be found in the best seats down front at the musical shows. And I will wager a nice purse that one hundred times more Catholics will have seen " Sailor, Beware! " than O'Neill's and Barry's plays grouped together. O'Neill, himself a Catholic, hasn't been in a theatre to see a play of any kind, Catholic or otherwise, since November 7th, 1918. And Barry, also a Catholic, spends most of the theatrical seasons happily sunning himself in Bermuda. Yet both — and O'Neill in great particular — imagine that, though they themselves do not go to the theatre, millions of their fellow Catholics will pile over one another jumping into taxicabs to crowd into theatres to see their Catholic plays.

When a Catholic wants Catholicism he either goes to church or stays at home and reads a pleasant echo of it in the novels of Willa Cather. When he goes to the theatre, he is no different from such of his mentors as the three good and excellent priests of Philadelphia who, at my late brother's dinner before his marriage to a dear Catholic girl, being asked what play they would like to go to the following evening — my brother had reserved boxes at the five decidedly various attractions then current in Philadelphia — as one man cried out, *"The Ziegfeld Follies!"*

Blackouts And Intermissions. — Shaw's remark that more theatregoers are bored by intermissions than ever were bored by plays applies as well to internal intermissions in plays. Nothing, as he has said, so lets an audience down as the customary act-intermissions. What success the moving pictures have enjoyed is doubtless at least partly due to the fact that they have done away with intermissions, play right through from beginning to end, and so sustain their audiences' mood and interest. But not only has the dramatic theatre persisted in its idiotic and ruinous custom of intermissions after each act of a play; it has, to boot, lately often increased the hazard of such intermissions by a long series of brief intermissions within each act of a play. I allude to the multiplying number of plays whose acts consist of many short scenes and which, to effect the necessary changes of scenes, intermittently either douse the lights or drop the curtain for a period of anywhere from one to two or three minutes. To demand of an audience that its mood be preserved in such circumstances is to demand the impossible. More plays have been killed by blackouts, frequently dropping curtains and intermissions than have been killed by all the destructive criticism since the theatre began.

Take, for example, a play called " Carry Nation," by one McGrath, not long ago offered to the local trade. It was, in truth, a poor attempt at chronicle drama setting forth the life and times of the illustrious saloon Hitler. But had it been a ten times better play, its two-minute blackouts between each of its fifteen scenes, to say nothing of two fifteen-minute intermissions added at due intervals for extra measure, would have knocked out completely the audience's interest. Intermissions may be well and good for trashy plays — the longer then, the better — but in the case of worthier plays they are simply the refuge of audience ignoramuses. Revolving stages and other such modern devices can handily do away with the old mechanical necessity for them. And the human rump which is competent to sit patiently and ungrumbling at a two-hour dinner party, a three-hour beer table or in a four-hour Pullman chair is perfectly competent to sit patiently ungrumbling in a two-hour theatre seat.

ᔈ ᔈ

Actors As Producers. — Although I do not suppose that many will too vociferously argue that nine-tenths of the general run of actors are not *Dummköpfe,* it occurs to one that many of the more interesting plays and productions would have been denied the American stage had it not been for the endeavor and courage of the remaining more estimable small fraction. The rank and file of managers and producers persistently ignored these plays and hesitated to make these productions. It was the actor Faversham who gave Stephen Phillips, with " Herod," his best hearing, as it was the actor Arnold Daly who introduced and fought for a hearing of George Bernard Shaw. It was the actor Miller who brought William Vaughn

Moody to the stage, and the actor Mansfield who brought "Cyrano." It was the actress Mrs. Fiske who encouraged the dawning better-grade American play three decades ago, and it was the actress Margaret Anglin who, in the midst of the prevailing managerial mush, deepened the stage with the Greek classics. It was the actress Grace George who brought over, and herself translated, some of the better modern French comedies; it was the actress Le Gallienne who gave a hearing to Jean-Jacques Bernard and Susan Glaspell, both unpopular playwrights; and it was an ex-Follies girl, Peggy Fears, who recently produced the best musical comedy that the local stage has had in many years. It was the actress Katharine Cornell who, though true enough she could see nothing in O'Neill's "Strange Interlude" when it was submitted to her, nevertheless produced Besier's "The Barretts of Wimpole Street" after exactly twenty-seven managers and producers had peremptorily rejected it. It was the actor Henry Hull whose interest alone made possible the production of the meritorious "Tobacco Road," as it was the actor Dennis King whose interest made possible the American production of the admirable "Richard of Bordeaux." The list might be extended indefinitely. And it has been and is the same, to an even greater degree, in England and France, from Lillah McCarthy up and down in the former to Gemiér down and up in the latter.

The Rape Of Obey. — André Obey's "The Rape of Lucrèce" is a simple and effective little play, touched occasionally with beauty and often with an original imagination. But no one who saw it when it was produced in America by Miss Katharine Cornell could possibly have suspected the fact. Laying hold of the modest little manuscript, Miss Cornell and her associates converted it into a "production" that needed only the late Florenz Ziegfeld lying in Lucrèce's bed to give the whole enterprise any glimmer of true meaning. So over-elaborate, so over-produced was the little play that the evening took on the impression of "In Egern on the Tegernsee" being played by the combined New York Philharmonic and Boston Symphony orchestras, with John Philip Sousa conducting.

Obey's small play, like his "Noé," was written for the semi-amateur company of fifteen actors who had taken up their home in Jacques Copeau's atelier in Paris. As produced both in the Vieux Colombier and, subsequently, at the Arts Theatre in London, it was treated exactly as it was intended to be, in the most innocent of stage styles, bordering closely on the amateur. I was told, indeed, that the play in its entirety was mounted for a sum considerably this side of one thousand dollars, and it looked it. But this very simplicity not only was what the play — as in the case of "Noé" also — absolutely demanded, but it accounted to no inconsiderable degree for its success with intelligent audiences. Yet what happened when it came under the wing of Miss Cornell and her American associates? Stupidly believing that the play was on its own account too slender a titbit for American audiences, the latter, in an effort to make a box-office show out of it, so figged it out with supervacaneous magnificent stage décor, narrators made up to look like statues designed for some prospective library building in Los Angeles, *de luxe* revue costumes, floodlights, spotlights and every other kind of light, and gaudy actors, that the poor little play was completely snuffed out under the rich avalanche.

From first to last, the little play didn't stand the ghost of a chance. Aside from a couple of fairly competent acting performances, it had everything done to it that Obey, in the throes of a nightmare, might have imagined. Even the translation by Thornton Wilder, who went collegiate-literary on this occasion with a vengeance, sedulously shovelled out of the original its every trace of written sincerity, charming artlessness, and dramatic ease. Of the top-heaviness of the stage investiture (beautiful, as is most of Robert Edmond Jones' work, on its own, but wholly inappropriate) and of the costumes that were right enough for an Erik Charell extravaganza but hardly for a morsel of a play like this, I have made note. But things didn't stop here. Enter the director. Under the impression that a naïve little play originally done by semi-professionals up a Paris side-street was meat for a very grave and very solemn occasion, this gentleman so directed it that it was surprising that the witty Mr. Deems Taylor, once he got a preliminary look at it in rehearsal, didn't wheezefully incorporate the Funeral March motif into his incidental musical accompaniment.

That, under these circumstances, the play proved a dismal fiasco, I need not record. It is something of a pity, for it deserved a better fate and would undoubtedly have enjoyed it had it been produced by less vainglorious hands. It was a success with critical audiences in Paris and something of an artistic sensation, moving the best of the London critics to high enthusiasm, when it was shown in England. In New York, it was simply something to evoke derision. As for the acting of the expensive local troupe, it nowhere, save in the creditable narrator reading by Robert Loraine, touched the competence of the French semi-amateurs. Miss Cornell's vocal moments were satisfactory enough, but in the direction of all-important pantomime a few lessons from even Miss Clara Bow would have helped the "first young actress of the American stage" considerably. Brian Aherne, as the lustful Tarquin, contributed to the rôle the externals of handsome matinée idol masculinity but, in the scene where he rapes the virtuous Lucrèce, with Miss Cornell's bland assistance suggested nothing so much — in the phrase of a certain New York producer — as a couple of Vassar girls playing pillow. The rest of the company, Loraine excepted, to quote the same producer, looked and acted as if they were playing "Cyrano de Bergerac" across the street, had run over between the acts to pay their respects to their colleagues, and had been caught on the stage unawares by the sudden rising of the curtain.

∽ ∽

Sample Directors.— A few minutes after the first curtain went up on "Come Easy" by Felicia Metcalfe, one of the characters alluded to a house which, he said, reminded him of a Swiss chalet (he pronounced it shallett), whereupon another character retorted that it reminded her of a Swiss cheese. A couple of minutes later, one of the characters exclaimed, "I've got an idea!", to which another, feigning astonishment and incredulity, ejaculated, "No!" Thirty seconds later, one of the characters referred to an Italian count, whereupon another observed that he'd bet he was no a-count. Later on in the proceedings, when it was established that the count was the genuine article, one of the characters allowed that "he always counted with me." The aforesaid count, I perhaps needn't add, was not without the inevitable white spats. He had been brought on to Baltimore by the young girl heroine, to stay with her family, directly after she had been briefly introduced to him at a wedding party in Philadelphia.

The stage director of this great masterwork, one Roberts, had evidently spent his life in the sole company of actors, in and out of greasepaint, and consequently quite naturally directed all the characters in the play out of their characters and into the semblance of actors. There was, true, little of characterization in the author's script, yet what little there was the directing gentleman eliminated in converting the actors into actors twice over. It would be a benefit to the theatre if many of these *soi-disant* directors would take a day off now and then, walk out of the stage door, stand on a street corner for a little while, and casually study a few human beings.

"The Blue Widow," by Marianne Brown Waters, proved to be another humdinger, falling under the general heading of what, long since, have come to be known as "widow comedies." I haven't the statistics at hand, but it is my guess that, excluding foreign importations and even the late Avery Hopwood figures, we have had in the last twenty years of American theatrical history fully five hundred plays of this particular species. There is little variation to them. Either the widow is a lady regarded with a certain amount of suspicion by the other women in the cast — there was that rumored affair with young Travis in Egypt, you will recall — or she is a lady whose quiet, worldly manner and easy sophistication (expressed in gently ironic remarks which are taken by the other women to be of sweet import) eventually make all the latter, who have been estranging their lovers or husbands, see the error of their ways. At other times, the widow, all honey on the surface, is a shrewd schemer underneath, or a playwright's mere repository for some feeble paraphrases of Wilde epigrams. But whatever she is, she is certain at the conclusion to capture through her wiles one or another desirable male in the cast upon whom one or more of her rivals have exercised an eye. Also, whatever the nature of the play, there is sure to be one scene in which the widow stands beside a piano and, toying with a long chiffon scarf, wistfully sings a little ditty, concerned either with amorous romance or, if the play be of a slightly saucy cut, with esoteric boudoir matters, the chorus in that case being sung either in French or in what passes on Broadway for English with a French accent.

The Mlle. Waters' contribution to the lack of joy of nations was composed for the most part of the recognizable stencils, including the husband whose wife doesn't understand him and who is therefore a come-on for the clever widow, the elderly, opulent and vain goat who mistakes the little widow's wide-eyed, baby-pouting gold-digging for genuine affection, the man-of-the-world who knows of the widow's past, together with his share in it, but does not betray her secret, etc. The manner in which the play was written suggested that the author had studied playwriting in Berlin about thirty years ago when the idea of an amusing popular comedy was to pair off the characters for two consecutive hours and have each pair successively repeat exactly the same scene. The stage director, one Winston, sharing the technique of his brother, Roberts, mentioned above, not only turned all the characters into actors given to the standardized actor comportment but, in addition, registered the play in so slow a tempo that he would unquestionably be a sensation if ever he went to China.

❧ ❧

The Deval And The Deep Blue Sea. — There is no news in the fact that French plays often suffer an attack of adaptational *mal de mer* when they come across the Atlantic and, accordingly, it will surprise no one that Jacques Deval's "Mademoiselle" was not quite so dramatically healthy in the version disclosed here as it was on its native soil. This local version was, true enough, considerably more faithful to the original than is usually the case but, nevertheless, things happened to it. Even had a spectator been unfamiliar with the virginal manuscript, he would have been more or less conscious that changes had been made in it, for there would have persisted in him a peculiar sense that something, even if he did not know just what it was, was a bit wrong somewhere.

This wrongness, he would eventually have deduced, lay in the character of the governess as edited in the American version. In the original, the character in question was a woman ridden by bitterness toward mankind. Consistently, undeviatingly, at least throughout the first two acts of the play, her hatred of men, who have cheated her of her every inner desire, and of women, who have had what she cannot have and who, even as periodically she has been drawn to them, have permitted men to take them from her watchfulness and care, controlled her every thought, feeling and act. The whole point of Deval's play rested upon this. Yet this hatred and this bitterness, in the American treatment, were attenuated and sentimentalized in the nonsensical effort to make the star actress' rôle somewhat more sympathetic to the local popular audience.

The play itself is a so-so comedy, though superior to a number that have been imported from France in recent seasons. That very relative shade of superiority seems to have merited a little consideration and protection. Certainly when the best moment in the play was sacrificed by a timorous adapter and leading woman to box-office sentimentality, the author has a right to complain, that is, if he has a pride that cannot be salved by mere box-office returns. The moment in question provides the curtain to the second act. In the original, the acrimony of the governess is brought to the boiling point when her young charge — who confides to her that she has, albeit illicitly, come by the one thing in all the world that the governess has dreamed of for herself, a baby — tenderly kisses her cheek. In a poison of rebellion and hatred the governess slaps her hand to her face and viciously wipes the kiss away. In that moment, the character of the woman is brought brilliantly to completeness. But what happened to Deval's governess here? When the young girl kissed her, she gazed tenderly after her as she left the room, permitted a hokum look of incipient mother-love to illuminate her features, and wistfully touched the place on her cheek where the buss was imprinted. In the words of Mr. Bert Lahr, I ask you!

CHAPTER XIII

Motion Picture Censorship

ᔐ ᔐ

The anti-censorship organizations have lately been making a beautiful noise about the threatened complete censorship of the motion pictures. The latter, they allege, will be fit only for juvenile half-wits when the scissors boys and girls, if they have their way, get through with them. An incipient art is to be hamstrung and squashed; free speech, the very foundation-stone of the Republic, is tottering; and so forth and so on. As a member of certain of these anti-censorship bodies and as one who, in almost all cases involving censorship, is ever ready to lend them his full and vigorous support, I nevertheless on this particular occasion privilege myself the pleasure not only of disagreeing with them, but of accompanying that disagreement with what, in the low vernacular, is known as the bird.

The current movie censorship drive, as everyone knows, is directed primarily against smut, with which the pictures in recent years have been brimming. Smut — and there is no other name for the thing the pictures have been retailing — is no part of any kind of art or even pseudo-art and its forced elimination should not concern any anti-censorship body with an ounce of intelligence left in its head. Furthermore, not *one* of the relatively better pictures made and released in the last fifteen years has in the least relied upon dirt and these pictures, while here and there censored in an unimportant detail or two under the former dispensation, have still remained possible for adult consumption and more or less intelligent enjoyment. What is more, these pictures have been the screen's high-water marks and some of them have made big money. To name a few: "The House of Rothschild," "The Private Life of Henry VIII," "Arrowsmith," "I Am a Fugitive from a Chain Gang," "Two Arabian Knights," "Tabu," "The Big Parade," "Disraeli," "Hallelujah," "Journey's End," "China Express," "The Hunchback of Notre Dame," "Variety," "Nanook of the North," "Potemkin," "Jeanne d'Arc," "The Man I Killed," "All Quiet on the Western Front," "The Last Laugh," "Two Hearts in Waltz Time," the several René Clair pictures, "The Birth of a Nation," "The Guardsman," "Hell's Angels," "Abraham Lincoln," "Cavalcade," "The Covered Wagon," "Little Women," "Public Enemy," "Broken Blossoms," various Chaplin films, "The Four Horsemen of the Apocalypse," etc. Still others such as "Ben Hur," "Way Down East," "Little Miss Marker," "Outward Bound," "The White Sister," "Smilin' Through," "The Champ," "Palooka," "Convention City," "The Thief of Bagdad," "Cimarron," various Pickford films, "Skippy," "Zoo in Budapest," etc., have been very successful and have been similarly uncensorable and uncensored save, in one or two instances, in negligible and entirely insignificant fragment. Furthermore, even under the strictest censorship, no films of any so-called educational or scientific value have been bowdlerized or damaged in the slightest, except perhaps one or two Bali or South Seas travelogues which have had a few feet of dark beauties' mammæ cut — and just where the great educational or intellectual value of amplitudinous bosoms lies, one has difficulty in making out.

The truth about the movies is that, in many cases, they have got to be so filthy that they do not in their present plight deserve the least consideration from any anti-censorship organization. As well let such organizations protest against the raiding of stag "smokers," prevention of the public sale of pornographic pink-backs, or the forbidding of promiscuous peep-shows. How the intelligence of a public is to be affronted and how its cultural rights are to be invalidated by eliminating from the movies scenes in which Mr. James Cagney pinches his old grandmother on the bottom, literary moments in which Mr. William Powell, surprised by an intruder while he and a lady are seated respectively on a water-closet and a bidet, jocundly observes, "That's all right; we're only chatting," and episodes in which Miss Mae West sardonically employs her spacious backside in lieu of repartee, I should like the anti-censorship crusaders, including those with whom in other directions I am whole-heartedly affiliated, to explain to me.

Censorship, far from hurting the movies (save in the pocket), in the long run will doubtless improve them. No first-rate, honestly made, intelligent picture is likely to be much interfered with. A few unimportant little cuts, now and again, perhaps, on the part of the inevitable busy-bodies, but of small impairment. Cheap smut, cheap humor, cheap sex — these will be compulsorily weeded out. Imagination, invention, better writing and a general greater literacy will perforce have to take their places. The notion that intelligent adults — or even children who haven't been dropped on the head, for that matter — take an overwhelming delight in guano seems to be a notion shared only and equally by the movie executives and the anti-censorship committees.

But, say these anti-censorship committees, it is not only smut and cheap suggestiveness that the censorship advocates are driving against; they are driving against what they are pleased to call the general " immorality " of the films. That is, everything from illegitimate babies and godless gangsters to prolonged kisses and facile divorces, from too accessible bedrooms and too inviting haystacks to women's bare thighs and undulating rears. Therein, they contend, lies the danger. All well and good. It is quite possible, even probable, that the motion picture censorship will now and again be as ridiculous as most censorship becomes when it gets a few free drinks under its belt and goes on a rampage. But that is not the point at which we are trying to get. The point — and we repeat it for the stubbornly obtuse — is that this violent free-for-all censorship movement would never have got under way if it had not been for the smut in which the movies have permitted themselves gloriously to wallow. The smut started the ball rolling and gave the censors the necessary ground into which to dig their indignant — and properly indignant, if we do say so — toes. If it had not been for the smut, things would have gone on in the old, easy, humdrum censorship way, and with little or no damage to the films. But the pictures have now got what was coming to them. With certain honorable minor exceptions, they have given the public excrement in return for its entertainment money, and the excrement has been brought home and dripped onto the parlor rug and the nursery carpet, and has befouled the household. And not only the pictures themselves, but the way in which they have often advertised themselves in the newspapers and the way in which they have heralded their appearance by means of suggestive and often disgustingly dirty " trailers."

Let the anti-censorship bodies face the facts and meditate them. All of us are against censorship, but those of us with some little sense left may reflect that there is a whale of a difference between reputable literature, reputable drama, and even reputable motion pictures on the one hand and foul money-grubbing dung on the other. To fight in behalf of such stuff is to lose the whole fight against censorship.

CHAPTER XIV

The Movies Take Over the Stage

∽ ∽

The news that the motion picture companies, operating in combination, have bought out the New York theatrical producers and taken over their theatres *in toto* for next season has naturally come as something of a surprise. There had been rumors, of course, but we smilingly and loftily had waved them aside, like so many week-end invitations to Quogue, L. I. The idea was unthinkable, unbelievable. Yet the fact now confronts us. On next September 1st, according to the announcements, the movie industry will be in complete control of the legitimate stage and its drama, with Mr. Irving Thalberg and Mr. Louis B. Mayer of the Metro-Goldwyn company, Mr. Samuel Goldwyn and Mr. Joseph Schenck of the United Artists and Twentieth Century companies, the Messrs. Cohen, Cohn, Cone, Coyne, Garfunkel, Katz, Satz, Zukor and Lustvogel of the Paramount company, and the Messrs. Selznick, Sheehan, Kraftsuppe, Laemmle, Ganzbrust, Franklin, Lasky and the eighteen Warner brothers of the various other companies as a board of governing directors and general overlords.

With this impressive array of names, the situation looks encouraging. It may be true that Mr. Goldwyn, in his own film field, took Zola's Nana and converted her into an Edward Childs Carpenter ingénue; it may be true that Mr. Thalberg took O'Neill's Nina Leeds and converted her into a virginal Florence Nightingale; it may be true that Mr. Katz, or whatever his brother-in-law's or uncle's or cousin's name is, took " Peg O' My Heart " and introduced scenes showing Peg dancing in her birthday clothes at a National Republican Committee stag smoker; but, after all, let us not forget that Mr. Gilbert Miller called Bourdet's " Le Sexe Faible " " The Sex Fable " when he produced it in New York, that Mr. Guthrie McClintic took Obey's simple little " Lucrèce " and made it indistinguishable from a Cecil De Mille production, minus only the omnipresent gay bathtub, and that the Theatre Guild, besides actually playing George O'Neil's " American Dream " backwards, has rejected as utterly unimportant and insignificant plays by O'Casey, Pirandello and — for many years —O'Neill in favor of the masterpieces of Dawn Powell, the Siftons, A. A. Milne and Mr. David Liebovitz.

As I say, the situation, despite the pitiful grunts and grousings of Mr. Brock Pemberton, who produces about one play in every three years, and of Mr. Percy Hammond, who has to come in all the way from Easthampton, Long Island, to review it — the situation, as I say, looks encouraging. Particularly when we peruse the preliminary plans of the movie executives.

According to the Hollywood announcements, the season will officially be opened with an all-star $350,000 revival of Verneuil's two-character play, " Jealousy." There will be eighty-five people in the cast, including Clara Bow, Jean Harlow, Carole Lombard, Toby Wing, Mae West, Joan Blondell, Anna Sten, Claudette Colbert, Conchita Montenegro, Dolores del Rio, Ginger Rogers, Myrna Loy, and a swimming pool. It has not yet been decided whether men will be included in the cast or not. Following close upon the heels of this colossal production will come Katharine Cornell's revised presentation of Shakespeare's " Romeo and Juliet," with Miss Cornell appearing in the nude. Basil Rathbone who, under the late theatrical dispensation, played Romeo to Miss Cornell's Juliet, will be replaced, by way of giving a little life and vitality to the stale classic, with James Cagney. The third presentation, due on September 26, is to be a new American drama, by Mr. Louis B. Mayer's brother-in-law, called " Sex!!! " It is possible, says the announcement, that the title may be changed to " Sex!! " but several conferences will have to be held before a definite decision is arrived at.

In October, we are promised four great productions. Norma Shearer, under the artistic personal direction of Mr. Thalberg, is billed to do Ibsen's " The Master Builder," rewritten by Ben Hecht and Charles MacArthur, with Busby Berkeley in charge of the choreography. Madison Square Garden has been leased for the presentation and Samuel Rothapfel, the beloved " Roxy," will have charge of the stage lighting and lobby decorations. Next will come an intimate musical romance with a cast of 700, to be produced in the Little Theatre. The rôle of the little orphan princess will be filled by Beverly Sitgreaves, while that of the amorous Grand Duke Adolpho will be played simultaneously by the Four Mills Brothers. If the Four Mills Brothers are occupied at the time making shorts, it is announced that their place will be taken by the Three Radio Rogues. Johnny Weissmuller is to have the rôle of the old crippled inn-keeper. Oscar Strauss will compose the score, which is to be rewritten by Gordon and Revel. During the second act, the whole audience will be moved up to the balcony that it may, from that point of vantage, enjoy a bird's-eye view of the chorus maneuvers and so not miss the Hollywood effects contrived by cameras swung aloft on derricks.

On or about October 18, Mr. Samuel Goldwyn will personally in the flesh supervise a big revival of Hall Caine's " The Christian," with a cast made up of all the Jewish actors who have been banned from Germany. Lest a propaganda purpose be suspected, the play will be given in Polish. A new airplane effect, the patent on which Mr. Goldwyn controls in conjunction with Mr. Howard Hughes, will be introduced to the public for the first time directly after the scene between John Storm and Glory Quayle in the third act. For the last week in October, a new American classic written in collaboration by the twenty-seven scenarists at the RKO studios is promised.

Its tentative title is " Adultery," though this, for censorship reasons, may be altered to either "Lechery" or "Rape."

November, however, will really see things get under way. What goes before, the movie people say, will be merely *hors d'œuvres*. The first week of this month will bring with it a sensation of sensations, to wit, a superrealistic revival of " Siberia," with Greta Garbo. It was at first also planned to use real snow and ice but this, under the circumstances, was abandoned as being sheer superfluity. As a treat following, we are to be given a fine novelty called "An Evening With The Stars." Booked for the Guild Theatre, the entertainment is to consist of personal appearances by ten rare film artists, to wit, Richard Dix, Buddy Rogers, John Gilbert, Clive Brook, Boris Karloff, Joan Crawford, Helen Twelvetrees, Zasu Pitts, Mitzi Green, and Lupe Velez. Mr. Dix will appear in an openfront white sport shirt, will frown intellectually in scholarly silence for ten minutes, and will conclude his performance by saying, "I want to thank all my loyal fans for the wonderful reception they have given me this evening. I feel mighty proud, I can tell you!" Mr. Rogers will play the saxophone for five minutes and beat on trapdrums for five more, all to a lovable boyish smile, whereafter he will step to the footlights (in this instance supplanted by a row of powerful navy searchlights) and say, "I want to thank all my loyal fans for the wonderful reception they have given me this evening. I feel mighty proud, I can tell you!" Mr. Gilbert will come on, nose and all, and vouchsafe the ladies in the audience twenty minutes of hintful and passionate, if somewhat regrettably fossilized, love looks, after which he will say, "I want to thank all my loyal fans for the wonderful reception they have given me this evening. I feel mighty proud, I can tell you!" Mr. Clive Brook will smoke a pipe and emulate Mr. Dix by frowning intellectually in scholarly silence for fourteen minutes, after which, being British, he will vary his colleagues' averments by saying, "I wish to thank all my loyal fans for the jolly reception they have accorded me this evening. I feel pretty jolly well set up about it, I say, I say!" Mr. Karloff will make himself up like a two-months-old corpse and will lie in state on the stage for eighteen minutes, the audience being privileged to pass in front of the bier and to touch and feel him. Being an artist who takes his art seriously and so not wishing to step out of the picture, Mr. Karloff will say nothing but will have an attendant, dressed as a grave-digger, pass out handbills informing the audience that he wants to thank all his loyal fans for the wonderful reception they have given him that evening and that he feels mighty proud, he can tell them.

Miss Crawford's part in the program will consist in a beauty lecture. She will show the ladies in the audience how, by the application of two quarts of tomato juice cocktails, a can of Sherwin-Williams carmine paint and a large brush dipped into a pail containing half a dozen old red flannel union suits, milady's mouth may be made to look like a lovely and tempting opened watermelon. After the lecture Miss Crawford will prettily and demurely thank her loyal fans for the wonderful reception they have given her. Miss Twelvetrees, who believes in the use of but *one* quart of tomato juice cocktails on her lips and who hence is ethereal, will pout sweetly at the gentlemen in the audience for ten minutes, thus inculcating in them an overpowering *Heimweh* for the Poillon Sisters, and Miss Pitts will open her eyes like a new baseball park and go in for wistfulness in a big way, after which both ladies will coyly finger their skirts and thank *their* loyal fans for the wonderful reception. Little Mitzi Green, who now weighs almost as much as Jim Tully, will come on in rompers and be very kiddy cutie, delighting the audience, as extra good measure, with a boop-a-doop song. Then she will lisp, "I wanna thank all my thweet fanth for thith wunnerful retheption." Finally, Miss Velez will appear and will give, in quick succession, nine imitations of an orthodox young Mexican woman imitating Hollywood's picture of an uncontrollable and devastating flood of yo-himbin. Miss Velez, breathless and exhausted by the strain of her efforts, and eager to put on her old-fashioned night-gown and have a nice hot glass of Ovaltine before going quietly to bed, will pause long enough to say in over-broken English, "Me wants to tank my frens for zis warnerful recepçion what zey have given me zis evening." It promises to be a big night, whatever Mr. Brooks Atkin-

[207]

son may say. Speaking for myself, I have ordered two new suits of evening clothes.

Another big November item will be a revised version of Bernard Shaw's " Back to Methuselah " with not merely the first but *all* of the scenes laid in the Garden of Eden. The Adam will be Buster Crabbe. There will be forty Eves. The following production, it is hoped, will be one of the real box-office sensations of the season. It will be a revival of " Little Women " which, you will recall, when done on the screen, was a gold-mine because of Katharine Hepburn's presence in it. In order to ensure an even greater box-office success on the stage, the movie executives will cast the play not only with Miss Hepburn, but with her entire family, including her father, mother, brother, sister, two uncles, three aunts, and former husband. Mr. Sid Grauman, of Grauman's Chinese Theatre, Hollywood, will be in charge of the première, a feature of which will be a two-hour preliminary concert in front of the theatre by Ozzie Nelson and his band, augmented by Freddy Martin and his, the combination to be led by Guy Lombardo.

The outstanding production planned for December will be the Wampas Babies in Brieux's " The Seventeen Daughters of M. Dupont," although there will also be a new play by Eugene O'Neill, rewritten by the well-known scenario writers, Riskin and Glasmon, in collaboration with King Vidor and the executives of the Columbia studios. The new year will be ushered in by Warner

Oland in a dramatization of all his Charlie Chan pictures. Performances will be continuous, the first show starting at 10 a.m. and the last at midnight.

Further plans for 1935 include a new play by John Monk Saunders for Sidney Blackmer, who will be supported by George M. Cohan, Walter Hampden and Walter Huston; a production of " Othello " with Stepin Fetchit in the rôle of the Moor; and a revival of " Zombie " with Theda Bara, Pola Negri, Nita Naldi, James Kirkwood, Lionel Barrymore, and Bronco Billy's horse.

CHAPTER XV

The Chaplin Buncombe

⁌ ⁌

1. Charlie Chaplin is a superior clown.

2. Charlie Chaplin is the most famous product of the Hollywood studios.

3. Charlie Chaplin is an international favorite.

4. Charlie Chaplin often combines with his humor the effective touch of pathos.

5. Charlie Chaplin is one of the few really expert pantomimists that the screen has developed.

1. *True.*

2. *True.*

3. *True.*

4. *True.*

5. *True.*

⁌ ⁌

1. Charlie Chaplin is a great artist.

2. Charlie Chaplin is a genius.

3. Charlie Chaplin is a great actor with infinite possibilities as a tragedian.

4. Charlie Chaplin is a great movie director.

5. Charlie Chaplin shows himself in the preparation of his pictures to be a highly imaginative scenarist and a skilful musician.

1. *Eliminate the adjective and heavily qualify the noun.*

2. *Bosh.*

3. *A limited actor with no possibilities as a tragedian.*

4. *Competent but certainly not great.*

5. *A sometimes moderately imaginative scenarist and a very shabby musician.*

∽ ∽

Now that we have had his picture, "City Lights," believed by Chaplin himself to mark the pinnacle of his talents in the various directions above named, some such critical stock-taking of his gifts and resources may be undertaken. Since he devoted three solid years of effort to the picture, it may — even without Chaplin's word for it — be held as a standard of more or less final judgment. In what light does it disclose him? It discloses him as still the ingratiating clown with a comedy routine that remains exactly the same as that displayed in his very earliest pictures. Its humor, edited by him, consists chiefly in a series of ancient "gags," such as the jocosity implicit in a stab in the seat, in the eating of paper streamers under the impression that they are spaghetti, in the adjustment of the thumb to the nose, in the accidental falling backward into a body of water and splashing around therein, in an inopportune attack of hiccoughs (on this occasion embellished with a whistle), in the pursuit of a cigar butt, and in the propulsion from a house of an unwelcome guest at the point of a toe. Its musical accompaniment, save for a few moments' burlesque of the talking pictures, amounts to nothing more than a cheap paraphrase of such past popular tunes as "Valencia" and the like. And its remarkably original and imaginative thematic thread of pathos — so lavishly praised by the journalistic enthusiasts — is discovered to be the long familiar motif dear to Max Maurey's Grand Guignol and the sentimental novelists and playwrights of a bygone day: the blindness which imagines it beholds beauty and, with the return of vision, finds to its own and another's heartache only the commonplace and the sadly ugly.

Through all this, Chaplin moves as he has always, without much variation of any kind, moved. He is still the fundamentally proficient zany that he was years ago, but so inelastic is his technique that his every movement, every grimace, every gesture, every eye-lift is foretellable a second or two ahead of itself. Every now and then in his career — or at least since he abandoned the high silk hat he used in his first picture and put on the funny little derby — he has hit upon a jolly or tender bit of stage business that has lent to his performance a momentary superficial aspect of novelty. But, in the main, his antics, often winning though they are, have followed a more or less established pattern.

The funniest moment in " Easy Street " was not Chaplin's, but the scene wherein a monstrous thug, walking down the street with a girl after committing murder, arson, mayhem and what not, suddenly reflects that he is walking on the wrong side of the lady and chevalier-like quickly changes his position. Certainly half the pathos touched with humor in " The Kid " was due to the performance in that picture of the then little Jackie Coogan. The monkeyshines of the fire department, rather than the tricks of Chaplin, constituted the most comical moments in " The Fireman," and the audience's loud shouts of mirth over the spectacle of Chaplin hanging on to the hut toppling over the precipice in " The Gold Rush " were evoked not by Chaplin but by a hired dummy. It would be interesting for a better memory than mine to plumb the various films further and determine just how much of their real humor or pathos was directly attributable to Chaplin's performances or to those of others. What is to be credited to Chaplin as a scenario-compiler or a director is apparently not always properly to be credited to him as an actor.

In " City Lights," Chaplin had a rich opportunity to make use of sounds, both for their own valuable collaborative effect and in the way of travesty, which he did not take advantage of. After the first few moments with their imitation of the talking screen's voices in terms of musical instruments — a fetching idea — there was no use of sound that was not stale and obvious. The imagination shown by René Clair, the French director, in " Under the Roofs of Paris," in such a situation, say, as that wherein the increasing volume of an approaching train accompanies the mounting anger and desperate combat of the two gangsters, was nowhere visible in the Chaplin film. The musical invention and humor divulged by the director of such a German picture as " Two Hearts in Waltz Time " were completely absent, as was the murderous talking picture burlesque of even some such third-rate Mack Sennett film as "A Hollywood Hero."

The newspaper hallelujah chorus, perhaps not altogether oblivious of the size of the advertisements and the consequent glee of the advertising departments, proclaimed " City Lights " and Chaplin — I quote literally — in the following terms: " superb," " incomparable, magnificent," " a dazzling pattern of comedy and pathos," " a great genius," " an artist without a peer," " killingly funny," " a very brilliant film," etc., etc. The picture and Chaplin were not any of these — and by a long shot. I should sum up the situation rather by saying that the picture was one of the poorest that Chaplin has made and that Chaplin himself, while still the best clown that the movies have bred, and while a pantomimist above the ordinary, is no longer, because of endless repetition, anything like so amusing as once he was. In plain fact, he is frequently a bore.

TO THE READER OF THIS BOOK:

It always gives me pleasure to keep you regularly informed about my new publications. If you are not already on my mailing lists, I should like to have you there. If you will check below the subjects of special interest to you, and drop this card in the nearest postbox (no stamp is necessary; I pay the postage), I shall send you our announcements regularly.

( ) Fiction - Continental writers (translations)
( ) Criticism, drama, essays, and poetry
( ) Philosophy and Social sciences
( ) Reprints of Classics
( ) Fiction - American and English
( ) History and Politics
( ) Biography and travel

( ) Business and Law
( ) Science including psychology
( ) Seasonal Catalogues
( ) Art and limited editions
( ) Mysteries and Adventure
( ) Music - biography and criticism
( ) Books for boys & girls

Borzoi authors of special interest to me: ....

Please fill in the following:

Do you buy your books directly from publishers? .... Do you buy in bookstores? .... if so, please indicate name of your bookseller...

NAME (Please print) ....

STREET ADDRESS ....

CITY & STATE...

ALFRED A. KNOPF, Publisher   730 Fifth Avenue, New York City

CHAPTER XVI

General Remarks

か か

1

It becomes increasingly evident as the seasons pass that fewer and fewer French boulevard plays are longer suited to the advanced American stage. Their once "worldly sophistication" has come to have a juvenile ring; and their sex capers, once looked upon as very wicked and daring, today impress local audiences as the essence of innocence. Beside something like " Tobacco Road," the amorous little epigram-embroidered copulations of the modern French drama have the air of kindergarten pranks. And beside something like " Sailor, Beware!" even the present-day Palais Royal farces are babies' rattles. What the presently bankrupt French theatre needs for its commercial salvation, apparently, is a good dirty mind.

2

Studying the acting performances on the local stage, one encounters an almost uniform deficiency on the part of the players. I allude to what may be termed the business of looking. While we always hear a great deal about the business of listening — that is, the convincing quality of an actor's attention and absorption in what is being said to him by another actor — the equally important business of looking — that is, a coincidental ocular attention and absorption — is seldom if ever remarked upon. Among all the players active in the American theatre at the moment, only George M. Cohan is in this regard believable and impressive. The rest listen more or less effectively, but none of them has learned the trick of co-ordinating eye and ear.

It is only recently, in point of fact, that the art of looking has received the slightest attention from our directors. And apparently with little success. The younger players do not seem to be able to catch the trick and, as for the old-timers, most of them still have " star eyes," eyes so vain of their owners' personal importance and theatrical eminence that they decline to lower themselves so far as to see (histrionically) any lesser person in the cast who is addressing them. The late Mrs. Fiske, you will readily recall, was a leading offender in this department. It was her acting custom not only never to give any sign that she ever heard what another character was saying to her but, in addition, to look at everyone on the stage as if he (or she) were a complete and rather odious stranger, and smelled a little to boot. Ethel Barrymore doesn't go that far, but she nevertheless gives one the impression of never seeing anyone who is speaking to her unless it be the leading man, and then her ocular appraisal of him has less to do with him as a character than with the kind of collar and necktie he happens to be wearing. So with most of the others, excepting Margaret Anglin and Grace George, the only two older players who do anything at all about "looking" with interest and conviction.

3

One of the apparently unavoidable weaknesses of drama is the arbitrary imposition upon it of devices, thoroughly tedious, that the novel is able to make short shrift of. The irksome quality of so much of drama is due to internal demands that its form cannot escape. In a novel the author is confronted, let us say, with the necessity of introducing to one another a number of characters who are meeting for the first time at a reception, dinner, or something of the kind. With the single phrase, " after the dull prefatory amenities were over," he is able to get down to business; there is no need for him further to waste time and space, no need for him to enervate his readers with unimportant and useless detail. But the dramatist, facing a like situation, must inevitably, because of the awkwardness of the peopled stage, dissipate time and fray the interest of his audience with a lot of empty dialogue that runs about as follows:

" How do you do, Mrs. Jones. You know Mrs. Smith, I believe? "

" Of course. So pleased to meet you again, Mrs. Smith.

Mrs. Smith, may I present my sister and my brother-in-law, Mr. and Mrs. Brown — Mr. and Mrs. Smith."

" I'm pleased to meet you."

" Thank you, and I'm pleased to meet you."

" Hello there, glad to know you, Brown! "

" How are you? "

" Why here's Bobby! "

" How are you? Hello, Mollie, how are you? "

" Bobby, you know Mr. and Mrs. Jones and Mr. and Mrs. Smith, don't you? Mr. and Mrs. Jones, Mr. and Mrs. Smith, this is Bobby — Mr. Robinson."

" I'm very glad to know you."

" How are you, Bobby? "

" Fine, thanks. Hello, Ed."

" You've met my husband, haven't you, Mrs. Jones? "

" Yes, indeed; it's delightful to see you again."

" So glad to see *you*. You and Mrs. Robinson know each other, don't you? "

" Hello, Hattie. And oh, Lucy! "

" Lucy, Mrs. Jones, this is Mrs. Brown, Mrs. Brown — Mrs. Jones, Mr. Jones, Mr. Smith, Mrs. Smith, Mrs. Robinson."

" I don't believe you've met Mr. Clark, Mrs. Robinson."

And so on . . .

The reader, suspicious of critical facetiousness, will doubtless put down the above as an exaggeration, designed for easy comical effect. Any skilful playwright, he will believe, would be able easily to avoid such tiresome and unnecessary routine. Yet the dialogue that I have quoted, save for the Smith, Jones and Brown nomenclature, follows very closely the dialogue in a recent stage success written by two of our most adept theatrical writers.

Another shortcoming of the drama lies in its necessity to do something with and about the characters who, though present on the stage, are for the moment unessential to its direct and immediate purpose. That is, characters who up to the moment have been concerned in the action but who, upon the entrance of another character and a colloquy between that character and still another, must temporarily be maneuvered to one side of the platform until they are again needed. In the novel such characters may be forgotten by the author; he need not concern himself with them until it is necessary again to bring them into focus. But in the drama, inasmuch as they remain right there in plain view upon the stage, the playwright must arbitrarily do something about them, however unnecessary to the drama itself they may temporarily be. He must, unless he be of the lazy and incompetent type who trusts everything to the stage director, devise silly, time-killing business for them, must write into his script half-articulate nothings for them to mumble (by way of keeping the picture "lifelike"), and must otherwise strain himself to conceal their perfectly obvious but unnecessary presence. In the novel, as I have observed, they may safely be left in the wings of the reader's imagination.

[219]

There is no dramatist, however dexterous and subtle, who does not find the pace of his play often naturally and unavoidably retarded for reasons that, so far as the pace of a novel goes, need never concern the novelist, however lacking in dexterity and subtlety. A novelist writes the line, " Mary got up from her chair, drew the blinds, put out the cat, locked the door, and turned down the lamp." It takes the reader exactly four seconds, by actual count, to read the line, ingest it and get the picture the novelist desires. A dramatist writes exactly the same stage direction in the present tense and by the time the actress playing Mary gets up from her chair, draws the blinds, puts out the cat (even if the beast be on this occasion sufficiently tractable), locks the door and turns down the lamp, at least four minutes have been consumed and the picture the drama-tist establishes is no whit more effective, from a dramatic-artistic point of view, than that established by the novelist in four seconds — assuming in each case, of course, that the episode is not particularly vital to the direct current of the novel or the drama. In almost every drama, any-where from fifteen to twenty-five minutes is thus wasted because of the concreteness of the stage and its personages; nothing is gained by the drama itself; what the novel naturally profits by both in pace and artistry the drama must compulsorily lose. Even the Expressionist drama, which tries to work itself down to a basic skeleton, does not altogether succeed in conserving such wasted time.

The stage has in late years become increasingly conscious of these and other deficiencies of the drama as opposed to the novel and has exercised itself to diminish their degree. In some directions it has succeeded, as witness the device of sudden blackouts and the quick fading of lights to take the place of too slowly falling curtains, the curtailment of elaborate stage directions, and the like. But there is still considerable imaginative distance to go before the drama may be its simple self and tell its simple story, as the novel tells its story, without suffering the interposition of foolish and wholly unnecessary, if indeed thus far apparently uncontrollable, mechanical and personal barriers. Smaller and shallow-set stages have done much to tighten exits and entrances and save wasted time in those directions; heightened directorial speed manages on occasion to quicken drama that antecedently moved too slowly; multiplicity of scenes (harking back to Elizabeth's day) have been resorted to in order to get into the drama some of the novel's flexibility; and other such stratagems have contrived to bring the drama a few paces nearer to the novel. But the rest still remains for tomorrow's inventiveness.

4

In any inquiry into the decline of occasional audience-interest in the present-day American theatre one factor — often esoterically discussed but because of its delicate nature withheld from print — cannot much longer remain out of type. It is a phenomenon that has appeared in the theatre within the last four or five years and that it has been instrumental in reducing to no little degree not only the persuasiveness of various plays and musical shows but the reaction, albeit often unknowingly, of their customers has for some time now not been lost upon certain of the producers and all of the critics. I allude to the increasing number of women players who are of the sexual disposition of the Aeolian-Greek island colonizers.

In the last few years numerous women of this Mytilene cast have come to the local stage and with their quickly felt, if not always consciously recognized, masculine hardness and chill undertone have made subtly ineffective and even ridiculous the plays and shows in which they have appeared. Love scenes have missed all fire and have become indistinguishable from those played in college shows by boys dressed up as girls. Glamour and sex stimulus, those two often critically disparaged but important assets of the theatre, have gone by the board. And musical shows, once of a piece with monkey glands, have been converted into so much saltpeter.

It is obviously impossible to set down names, places and dates, but it might easily be done. Anyone who knows the local theatre would have no difficulty in doing so. Such a catalogue would suggest to many audiences, even if they have not realized before what it was that failed to inveigle them in the case of a certain play or show, the very probable nature of the phenomenon that brought about their emotional disablement. Such a catalogue would recall to them a certain Shakespearean revival whose passionate beauty had all the compelling fervor of an ice-bag, a comedy of wistful love with the flavor of Berlin's Monokol night-club, a sentimental French play whose heroine needed only a pair of trousers to double as the hero, a musical revue whose leading danseuse made a bag of nails seem as soft, in comparison, as a bath sponge, a fantasy from the Italian that took on, in its delicate leading feminine rôle, the aspect of a speakeasy bouncer dressed by Callot, an Ibsen revival whose star actress would have driven old Henrik straight into the arms of the chatelaine of the *Für Damen* at the Café Luitpold, a tender little comedy in which, when the leading woman kissed the leading man, he obviously felt like an androgyne, and still another exhibit in which one of the conspicuous women members of the cast played a scene of amorous passion with the leading male actor as if he were a leper.

I appreciate that there is something refractorily comical about any such subject as is here being exposed to print. But there is nothing comical about it when one considers the plays that are being castrated and the box-office that on many occasions is being forsaken. It is, plainly enough, not a case of morals; it is simply a case of unfitness for certain jobs. These women who bask in latitude 39° North, longitude 26° 20′ East, may be excellent workers in other fields of human enterprise, but they do not belong on the stage of warm, throbbing and convincing drama nor on the sex-appeal music show platform. Audiences, with their vague dissatisfaction, their inability — with all the willingness in the world — to respond to the dramatist's invoked emotions, and their discontent with many an otherwise at least partly meritorious play, have proved and are proving that. Audiences may not know, but they feel. And even though not clearly knowing, they yet feel that something is wrong. You cannot cast Sappho as Cinderella, or as Juliet.

In a recent issue of the programs distributed in the New York theatres, one read, in the pages devoted weekly to the well-known figures of the theatre's yesterday, this paragraph:

" In Hyde Park, one day early in this century, Viola Allen remarked on the absence of butterflies (or so, at least, the story goes) and her companion immediately set about having things fixed. On the following morning a great flock of the dainty creatures was let loose in the park and by the next year a butterfly farm had been established and thousands of butterflies were being released in parks all through London. Miss Allen was that sort of woman. Her success, according to one reviewer, was ' largely one of personality, of charm, of that womanliness that always is content to go about in skirts.' "

The theatre today hasn't any pressing need of butterflies, but it could stand a lot more women like Viola Allen.

5

One of the obvious deficiencies of our current theatre is that so many of its plays are not being written by playwrights. We engage any number of young men with the right dramatic materials who are unable to put them into the dramatic form and an almost equal number of older men with the wrong dramatic materials, materials stale and hollow, who are gifted in putting them into the dramatic form. It is a pity that the two groups cannot get together.

6

Sometimes, when a young man realizes that it is not within his gifts to write a play with any body to it, he will artfully attempt to conceal his incapacity by writing a play completely devoid of body, in the fond belief that a vacuum will be less a vacuum if the intention to make it a vacuum is duly forestated. This is doubtless the procedure that was followed by Mr. Romney Brent in the composition of " The Mad Hopes." It is, however, a sorry matter that the composition of a play wholly devoid of body and yet entertaining is quite as difficult a job — even a more difficult one, indeed, — than the contrivance of a play possessed of body. The balancing of a light celluloid ball on the tip of one's nose imposes a greater dexterity than the balancing of a billiard cue.

To confect a play whose entire motivation rests upon madness and wit and sparkle calls for something akin to genius. Although any number of more recent playwrights have tried to negotiate the feat, the number who have succeeded is almost invisible to the critical eye. Among the American writers, only two, Harry Wagstaff Gribble in " March Hares " and Zoë Akins in " Papa," have come anywhere near to hitting the mark. Mr. Brent has missed the bull's-eye by several thousand miles. A play purposely and even violently empty of intelligence must none the less imply a very sharp grade of intelligence hiding around the corner. " The Mad Hopes " betrays hardly a juvenile intelligence hidden anywhere. A play that relies upon an impish humor to conceal its lack of content must have some degree of that humor. The impish humor of " The Mad Hopes " consists of such jocularities as a query as to the Scotch ancestry of one of the characters, with the latter's retort that he is usually full of it, and the observation of an American that, now that he has been enjoying a holiday in Europe, he is going back to rest. A play that calls for a high grade of wit if it is to live on the stage at all must have at least a semblance of wit. And the wit of " The Mad Hopes " finds its springboard in such ancient wheezes as relate to Ford automobiles and the Queen of England's hats.

Mr. Brent, being an actor, suffers from most of the other inevitable shortcomings of the average actor when he constitutes himself a playwright. His dialogue is less dialogue, in the accurate meaning of the word, than so many individual lines for individual and isolated actors. It is like a set of railroad tracks, minus only the glint and gleam, that go on and on, yet never meet or cross. It consists, in each separate instance, of a single actor's, or character's, part, with little reference to the other actors or characters. Also, the actor-playwright's regard for what he imagines to be a moneyed box-office is noticeable in such hokum devices as the handsome and generous Jewish *deus ex machina*. Also, one observes the over-elaboration of the actor's love: exits and entrances. No, airy brilliance is not to be achieved in any such manner. All that we get is the spectacle of a young playwright running madly around a stage, inflicting upon himself the indignities commonly associated with the *genus Anatidæ,* and loudly proclaiming that he is Oscar Wilde.

7

With negligible exception, the musical comedy made from a play is as dispiriting as the novel made from a play or wine made from a brick. Why anyone should want to take a play that usually was dull stuff in the first place and waste many thousands of dollars trying to persuade audiences that it is a gay show by the dubious expedient of having one of the male characters periodically deject himself upon his rear and another intermittently pinch one of the female characters in her exiting anatomy is just another of the many riddles that entertain a reviewer who has sense enough to keep his own money in the bank. Yet year in and year out the gentlemen of the theatre continue thus to make Chile bonds seem relatively a wonderful form of investment. What adds to the puzzle is that they seldom pick on a good play to serve as the book for their musical comedy, but pretty generally — with unearthly cunning — manage to select something that, when it was shown on the legitimate stage, chloroformed the interest not only of most of the professional reviewers, but made many of the more reputable lay customers hurry right over to the News-Reel Theatre.

The answer that the gentlemen in question customarily make, lifting their voices so that they can be heard above the champing of the storehouse-dray horses, is that good original books are hard to find and that as a consequence they have to fall back upon old plays willy-nilly. While there is surely something to be said for the difficulty of getting hold of good original books, there is nevertheless very little to be said for the necessity of falling back upon the kind of plays that they usually fall back upon. There are some plays that, while they might not make good musical shows, would at least make much better ones than the kind the gentlemen currently manufacture. But do they exercise themselves to find these more suitable plays? The answer is identical to the answer to the question: Wouldn't you rather have a brunette? Just as it was a sound stroke of showmanship to take "Old Heidelberg" and turn it into a musical show, as the play was essentially well suited to the musical form, so might there be some judgment in doing the same thing with Ludwig Fulda's old play, "Friends of Our Youth," or Jerome K. Jerome's "The Great Gamble," or Max Beerbohm's "The Happy Hypocrite," all more or less naturally fitted to the musical medium and all, incidentally, rather promising from both a box-office and critical point of view. But those aren't the kind of plays that the gentlemen think of.

8

One of the greatest problems presently confronting American playwrights is the impossibility of casting their plays when it comes to the rôles that call for juveniles. That is, young male actors. There are, true enough, available several very competent young men for the "Last Mile" type of play, the hard, brash, gutter species of drama, and one or two, as well, for the tough, slangy, curbstone species. But for the romantic, the sentimental, the polite, the intellectual, the literary, the glamorous, or any similar kind of drama, the field is barren. Things have come to a pass, in point of fact, where unless a young Englishman is to be had for such a rôle, the production may just as well be cancelled.

9

One of the more striking inadequacies of much of present-day American comedy writing is what may be termed the line fixation of many of our younger playwrights: the grim intentness upon the achieving of tart and saucy lines and the coincidental overlooking of the fact that such lines, however spirited and humorous in themselves, need a play to sustain them and give them value. The average young spark in our playwriting midst seems to imagine that if he can devise a number of lines that would evoke considerable merriment at a dinner table all that is necessary to constitute a play out of them is to hire some actors to speak them from a theatrical stage. The result is a series of white-face minstrel shows that, while here and there momentarily diverting, are no more plays, in any sound critical sense, than Lew Dockstader's shows were.

Perhaps as good a definition of a satisfactory play as any is a play the after-glow of whose wholeness persists in one as one leaves the theatre. These slick-line peppered exhibitions, without play body, may transitorily amuse while one is in one's chair, but even as the final curtain is tumbling down nothing of them remains in one's memory, and nothing of them accompanies one out to the door. They are like steamer acquaintances of a day, for the moment moderately entertaining and serviceable as cursory time-killers, but agreeably forgotten and never given a second thought the minute one docks. A real comedy playwright designs his comedy first and his lines afterward. Too many of our local youngsters work the other way 'round.

10

To succeed commercially in the theatre these days, a treatment of the old Cinderella theme must be either very good or very bad. When a critic makes any such observation as this, it is the habit of dolts, for all its truth, to put it down either to a straining for showy paradox or as mere

[230]

senseless smart-aleckry. Yet any one who knows his theatre will appreciate, from a scrutiny of the records, that it comes pretty close to being a fact. It is obvious that any very good paraphrase of the Cinderella theme — or, for that matter, any other theme — stands an excellent chance of success in the theatre. What is not in this case so obvious, although equally truthful, is that a very poor treatment of the Cinderella theme, above all other themes, stands the same excellent chance. Consider, for example, such more recent frumpy treatments, and their happy reception, as have been instanced in the cases of " A Church Mouse," " The Good Fairy," *et al.*

Mr. Sampson Raphaelson was the latest playwright to tackle the paraphrasing job. His effort was called " The Wooden Slipper." But, as he managed the job neither badly nor well enough, his play got nowhere with the box-office and went to the storehouse in less than a week. It is Mr. Raphaelson's misfortune that his mind has a penchant for the dramatic clichés of twenty years ago; doubtless due to his relatively tender years he gives every appearance of relishing them as something either wistfully or hilariously new. For example, he rolled on his dramatic tongue, in this last exhibit of his, that venerable cutlet of a hundred-odd plays of two or more decades ago consisting of the scene in which the lovelorn girl, suddenly learning of her swain's interest in another, inquires heart-brokenly whether he has told the other that he loves her; in which the swain remains mute and guiltily hangs his head; in which the downcast young woman thereupon also hangs her head (the twain maintaining the business for a full thirty seconds); and in which the young woman then abruptly moves over to the grand piano, stands erect and magnificently self-contained at its side, and imperiously informs him that he had better leave the house, the swain thereupon, after a shame-faced parting glance, making his exit with his head still down on his second waistcoat button. For another example, Mr. Raphaelson displayed a taste for extracting prolonged comedy out of the equally ancient dialogic device of having several characters attempt elliptically to describe a succulent dish which baffles their powers of precise gustatory specification. If in the future he wishes to make a deal of money at the box-office, Mr. Raphaelson will either have to write even worse than that — or a thousand times better.

II

In one of his comedies, the late Avery Hopwood made the observation that, however late one got to the opera "Siegfried," there was always one more act. In the same way, however late one gets to a Negro musical show, one is certain never to miss anything, as most of the acts, songs, dances, skits and turns are endless duplicates of one another, and with hardly any noticeable variation. Two things about almost any such show are inevitable: (*a*) that the second act, by virtue of its likeness to the first, is wholly unnecessary, and (*b*) that every one of its sketches is always exactly twice too long.

It would take a pretty memory to recall a Negro musical show devoid of any or all of the following ingredients: *1*, a street scene in which a policeman gets into a brusque altercation with a small Negro comic possessed of a plaintively humorous vocal squeak; *2*, a brace of male buck and wing dancers in white silk shirts, their hair glistening with bear-grease, who work themselves up to a frenzied hoofing pitch; *3*, a mixed troupe of spirituals singers clad in calico and overalls (Personal note: I herewith call for a rising vote on an indefinite moratorium on all spirituals); *4*, a sentimental song — with every third or fourth line ending with the word *baby* — sung by a man and woman the while they mosey back and forth in rhythmical slow motion; *5*, a sketch in which a portly female dinge entertains a large buck in her boudoir and is suddenly surprised by her husband who was thought to be in Baltimore, the aforesaid husband being the peewee comedian; *6*, a song and dance number in which the chorus girls are dressed as Pullman porters; and *7*, an act finale in which, to the accompaniment of some ear-deafening boiler-plant cacophony from the orchestra, the whole troupe, with little reason, kindles itself into a mad song and dance paroxysm.

12

Each new season provides us with examples of the progress that American comedy writing is making. It was not so long ago that — following the late Clyde Fitch's explorations of the female soul, so to speak, in terms of the fashionableness of the lingerie that covered it — the greatest heights that American-made polite comedy reached were paraphrases of "Divorçons" or transcripts of the British Alfred Sutro-H. V. Esmond kind of thing, with the scenery painted to look like Westchester. What smeared the stages were largely plotty vacuums that sought to posture as modish comedy on the score of a tea-cart, a butler, and a bell that pulled with a wall-cord instead of being operated by vulgar electricity. The stories were usually pretty much of a piece: either wives who, by the exercise of patience, tact and charm, succeeded in winning back their errant husbands from mistresses who, in a third act scene with the wives, revealed themselves in their true sordid colors; or husbands with errant wives who epigrammed the latter's lovers into eventual discomfiture and thus cleared the stage for a final scene in which, with the lights out, they felt their way back once again to the doors of their penitent wives' boudoirs, left hintfully ajar. Such borrowings and frauds are rapidly disappearing from our theatre, driven out by the new and welcome order. What we are now getting is some contact with life, and in place of the old characters who ever remained Frank Worthings and Margaret Dales under their grease-paint, characters of some authenticity and blood.

13

One of the faults that the critical boys have found with the various productions of anti-Nazi plays is the engaging of Aryan actors to play the rôles of Jews. If they are right on that score, down into the critical wastebasket go all the excellent Christian actors who have played Shylock and most of the Jewish men and women players, including Sarah Bernhardt, who have played everything from the Prince of Denmark and the young Duke of Reichstadt to Madame Butterfly.

14

I permit myself a critical meditation on what is in danger of becoming a disturbing technical monkeyshine on the part of Mr. Jerome Kern and whichever librettist he fetches unto himself. I allude to the labored casualness, the strained air of haphazardness, with which the musical numbers are presented. It was an effective, a very effective, trick at first, but with repetition it is getting to be a bit obvious and just a bit bogus. The notion of starting a song and then, just as its lilt and melody are swinging you into their grip, causing the singer to stop abruptly, light a cigarette and observe that he is sorry but he has to keep a date at Jack and Charlie's, in time gets a little on your nerves. As does the interruption of a lovely song, after the eighth or tenth measure, by having the lady vocalist halt suddenly and, for no sound dramatic reason other than a conceivable uncontrollable call of nature, rush out of the room. Then, too, I don't know about the value any longer — now that the device has become familiar — of having a serving maid, who has been buried all evening, or of a stagehand or someone else who hasn't been seen all evening, stroll languidly out on to the stage around 10:40 and purl the best song in the score. It smacks too much of the old-time football stratagem of bringing the village blacksmith into the game in the last minute of play.

15

There are probably not more than a handful of persons left in America (critics included) who any longer take much interest in acting as an art, and even those who do, seldom recognize and distinguish real acting when they see it. I refer you, if you are skeptical, to the common ecstatic appraisals of second-raters and the bland condescension to certain first-raters on the part of these folk. Ours is no more an actors' theatre but a dramatists'. Every now and again, to be sure, some actor comes along and, like Mr. Henry Hull, startles and overcomes lethargic criticism in his department by covering his still moderately youthful face with a crêpe whisker, walking with a George M. Cohan slouch, injecting into his vocal delivery a Hamtree Harrington squeak, and so presenting a very excellent approximation to a portrait of a Georgia cracker, and every now and again some actress appears and, like Miss Helen Hayes, accomplishes a similar end by giving a highly competent performance of Rose Trelawney in the rôle of Mary Stuart, but in the general run of things the day of audiences' and even critics' intelligent concern and enthusiasm for the actor's art seems to be, at least for the time being, past.

Consider, if you remain doubtful, the situation on the local stage of last season. Who — apart from the Mr. Hull and the Miss Hayes alluded to, and, of course and properly, Mr. George M. Cohan — were the players who attracted the greatest notice from audiences and, either immediately or reflectively, the critics? I give you the list. Tonio Selwart, in "The Pursuit of Happiness," a pretty young fellow from Central Europe and an Aryan paraphrase of Francis Lederer, who substituted an ingratiating manner and a pleasantly strange accent for any discernible real acting ability. Polly Walters, in "She Loves Me Not," a cutie who looked even cutier with half her clothes off. Elisha Cook, Jr., in "Ah, Wilderness!", a satisfactory juvenile, but surely nothing suggestively much, at the moment, beyond that. Bruce Macfarlane, in "Sailor, Beware!", a good-looking very bad actor. Basil Sydney, in "The Dark Tower," a player of considerable talent (recall his Hamlet) who was praised no end on this occasion simply because, at one stage in the proceedings, he disguised himself with a make-up that deceived perhaps one-half of the audience. Mr. Sydney, who is an actor with some critical sense, was doubtless the first to chuckle over the tributes to his art which should properly have been bestowed upon a childishly easy manipulation of a blond

[237]

wig, some pink grease-paint, and a Joe Weber belly mattress. Roland Young, in "Her Master's Voice," who, giving a good comedy performance, nevertheless gave exactly the same comedy performance, without the slightest variation, that he has been giving for years both on the stage and in the motion pictures. J. Edward Bromberg, in "Men in White," because he was the mouthpiece of the author's more noble sentiments, spoke them in much the same throaty Wilson Barrett tones that have led the same persons to regard Lionel Barrymore as a sterling artist, and remained immobile, à la William Gillette, while the action and loud talk swirled tumultuously around him. Mary Morris, in "Double Door," who, in the rôle of the grasping and venomous spinster villainess, spoke and comported herself from the first to the last curtain like a zombie out of the old Drury Lane melodramas. And Laurence Olivier, in "The Green Bay Tree," who looks exactly like two or three hundred head of movie Colmans, Asthers, Lowes, Rolands, Baxters, Boles, *et al.*, and acts exactly like them, thus affecting the ladies in exactly the same way and spot.

Who, in addition, evoked the audience and critical applause in the earlier months of the season? I give you that list as well. Miss Jean Arthur, a disturbingly attractive young woman, in "The Curtain Rises," who may hardly yet be said to be anything more than a disturbingly attractive young woman who may some day possibly be an actress. James Bell, a competent actor, in "Thunder

On The Left," who, absurdly cast in an absurd rôle, was admired for not being able to do anything in an acting way with it. Miss Florence Reed, in "Thoroughbred," for making up as a hobbling old woman, squatting on a sofa, and pointing her every acidulous remark by thwacking each passing member of the company across his posterior with her walking stick. A little girl named Jean Rouverol, in "Growing Pains," for acting like a little girl named Jean Rouverol. Miss Mady Christians, in "Divine Drudge," an actress of experience and skill, because — while she had no slightest opportunity to employ her experience and skill — she nevertheless looked beautiful. And, finally, though this is perhaps a not altogether fair example, Miss Miriam Hopkins, in "Jezebel," who — while it was pretty generally agreed that her performance was negligible — nevertheless aroused such enthusiasm with her magnificent frocks and golden hair that at least one critic whooped her up as a combination of Rachel, Rejane, Bernhardt and Duse.

16

Too many of the plays that one encounters in the current British theatre suffer from what may be described as a dramatic green-carnationism. The young men who write them are sometimes clever, sometimes moderately witty, and pretty generally literate, but their point of view is usually pink, and always superficial. Their plays have an unhealthy air. Conceal it though they may assiduously

[239]

try to, there is nevertheless to them the smell of something just a little bit sickly and foul. A peculiar perversity, like a feminine sneer, permeates them. The quiet, unassertive, but sure masculine quality is missing and, in its stead, there is either a counterfeit muscularity — cynicism in lace shorts — which hoodwinks no one, or a brazen affirmation of masculinity's lack. Some of these plays are fairly amusing, as a female impersonator is occasionally in a refractory vaudeville way amusing, but none of them is — I cannot think of a more pointed phrase — healthily comfortable. The good Lord knows that American popular drama is nothing for us to get patriotic about; as a matter of fact, it is often inferior in relative quality to the English. But, whatever may justly be credited against it — and that is considerable — no one can deny its ruggedness. It has a vigor, a blood beat, and an open directness whatever else it has not. There is, in a manner of speaking, a strength to it, whereas in the English equivalent there is a suspicious pallor, a taint of rottenness. And that taint becomes all the more evident when it is felt across the footlights of a crude but robust alien stage.

17

In Ronald Gow's "John Brown," what we engaged was an effort to relate the tale of the martyr of Harper's Ferry in the last year of his life, but one that was fatefully handicapped both by an insufficient skill in playwriting and by a dramaturgical ingestion of some of the sourest devices of the bygone stage. We accordingly began to fear the worst when, not more than ten minutes after the first curtain went up, little Ellen Brown sat her dolly in a rocking-chair and proceeded for a considerable spell to enter into a rapt conversation with it, and when, about three minutes later, Uncle Jeremiah's arrival surprised the family out of its wits by virtue of that old schnitz'l of hokum: the circumstance that one of the sons had forgotten to give the old boy's letter, absent-mindedly put into his pocket two days before, to his mother. This sort of thing cracked the play over the head at intervals throughout the evening, culminating in the last act in such cobwebbed dodges as several characters' nervously alarmed speculation as to the identity of a knocker at the door, when the audience knew perfectly well that the knocker was no one to be even slightly alarmed about — to say nothing of our ancient friend: the symbolic thunderstorm.

A good play on John Brown — or on John Smith or John Jones, for that matter — is not to be written in that way. But even if it were, the performance contributed to the leading rôle in this one by Mr. George Abbott would have pretty well wrecked it. Magnificently and appropriately made up in the memorable Brown whiskers, Mr. Abbott took the celebrated historical figure and gave him so thin a little voice and such wooden gestures that, at the conclusion of the performance, one confidently expected to see Vittorio Podrecca come out and take an acknowledging bow. What is more, Mr. Abbott privileged himself such a wealth of sanctimonious Morris Gest biblical play attitudes that one equally expected to have Signor Podrecca followed by a parade of camels.

18

In all the learned library of essays on the art of acting I sadly miss one on the histrionic virtuosity of dogs. I have read essays, even thick books, on every species of actor from human to marionette, but never have I encountered one on the undeniable genius of the canine. That dogs, like very young children, very old Germans, and most Negroes, are strangely gifted stage artists is obvious to anyone who has ever studied their various performances. A skilful child actor may prove a dud when he grows up; a skilful old German may have been something pretty bad up to the time he reached sixty-two; but a dog, once he gets on the dramatic stage, is an artist from puppydom until Equity buries him. Most actors, even the best, at one time or another give sorry accounts of themselves, but has there ever been a mutt on the stage who let down his art for a moment? Some of the performances that linger most beautifully in the critical recollection, indeed, have been those by dogs like the one who played in Frederick Ballard's "Young America." Some of the performances that linger most horribly in the same recollection have been those by human actors like some who played in the same play.

One of the gravest consequences of a war is the sentimentality over the late foe which engulfs a nation. This sentimentality, often assuming absurd proportions, is in direct ratio to the acquired peculiar distaste for the nation's late allies. The theatre, being the mirror of a people's prejudices, served aptly in demonstrating how far the aforesaid sentimentality went in the case of the Germans and Austrians, not only in this country but in England, too, and even in France. As I wrote while serving as an ambassadorial reviewer in London several years ago, the sentimentality of the English for their late enemy reached the point where about the only persons in London who weren't speaking with affectionate German inflections were the German headwaiters in the fashionable restaurants and night clubs. The theatre in London at that time was given over so widely to German matinée idols, Tyrolean shows, German singers and beery waltz music that, if a traveler wished to see anything English, he had to go to Berlin to satisfy his craving. Richard Tauber was drawing thousands of cheering Britishers to Drury Lane, Francis Lederer was knocking duchesses cold at the Lyric, musical shows like " The White Horse Tavern," with casts dressed in green suspenders and Bavarian shorts, were inducing in the English populace a wholesale nostalgia for pretzels and curled radishes, and tender little *Lieder* about the linden trees, the *Mädel* of

the Kurfürstendamm and the shadows of the Schwartz-
wald re-echoed whistlingly from innumerable stages
through the windows of the sedate old codgers' clubs in
Pall Mall.

Following close upon the complete cardiac surrender
of the Londoners came the sweet capitulation of the Americans and the French. Here, the big marmalade boom got
under way with "Sweet Adeline," a native confection
whose stage progress was applaudingly held up for almost
half an hour every night when Mr. Robert Fischer came
out and sang a schmerzy little ditty in German attesting
to the sad and beautiful sadness and beauty of something
or other sadly beautiful in Germany. The sentimentality
thus duly inaugurated gradually took on the volume of a
lovely brewery explosion and it wasn't long before it was
almost impossible to discover a play in which, at one
period or another, either an old German character didn't
take out his heart and let the audience see all the gold in
it or a slightly younger Austrian, usually a composer of
waltzes mournfully condemned to corrupt his art in Hollywood, didn't agreeably hold up the action for at least
ten minutes expatiating on the charm of the girls in the
Prater. With the musical shows, it was the same. Every
other one disclosed a complete Knox factory output of
Tyrolean hats, scenes showing little houses with red and
purple roofs on the distant green hills, and enough Viennese *Heimweh im drei Viertel Takt* to break an audience's
composite heart. In Paris, things came to the point where

the applause for the Busch family at the Cirque Medrano was so ecstatically vibratory that they could hardly retain their grip on their trapezes. And in the same season I saw in Paris with my own eyes a theatreful of young French women melt like so many amorous caramels before the heat of a Berliner with a little singing quaver in his larynx. The whole business came to such a pass, indeed, what with all this Hunny Boy stuff, that any play that disclosed its actors with long trousers on and its actresses without flaxen braids — and that did not contain a scene wherein a group gathered around a piano at twilight and sang "Röslein auf der Heide" — was a very welcome novelty.

20

After many years of theatregoing, I still can't make up my mind whether most actors act and talk like Englishmen or whether most Englishmen act and talk like actors.

21

Penetrating the lovely parsleys and croutons with which Mr. Gilbert Miller characteristically garnished the dish, one found Lajos Zilahy's "Firebird" just another slice of Hungarian ham. More and more it becomes plain that the Hungarians, who once — and not so very long ago — promised to be the life of the theatrical party have gone to seed. Nothing that has come out of that quondam lively play-mill in the last half dozen years has been worth talking about. Molnár, the only even faintly juicy play-wright left, has produced one or two moderately amusing trifles, but some time since has given unmistakable evidence that he, along with the others, has shot his bolt.

It is a melancholy picture. There was a day when the Hungarians indicated a wit and imagination that promised much, and actually and concretely afforded much, to the lighter stage of the world. At least five of the Buda-Pesth writers seemed to be fellows of considerable spirit, combining much of the sound gayety of the French comedy school with a measure of the thoughtful sobriety of the German and the sensitiveness of the Austrian. But what has become of them, and of the writers who have followed them? Nothing. Almost everything that they and these others have turned out in recent years has been little more than a paraphrase of the stalest boulevard comedy or the stalest problem drama of the Eighteen Nineties. Zilahy's play is an example. In essence, it is simply a re-working of the materials of such ancient balderdash as " Mrs. Dane's Defense," almost totally devoid of humor and entirely devoid of even a suggestion of fresh fancy.

In the last six years, I have either seen or read dozens upon dozens of Hungarian plays and, aside from the Molnár vaudevilles mentioned, there has not been one that was not a carbon copy of a carbon copy. Nowhere in any of them was there any sign of the originality and power and humorous ingenuity that one looked for and often found in the Hungarian drama of antecedent years. It is too bad. Another mine that seemed to have a little gold in it has proved to be just a hole in the ground.

22

On the theatrical Index Expurgatorius, it is high time that the following be listed: (*1*) operettas that have to do with a handsome, sadistic huzzar, who, at the climax to the second act, suddenly breaks off the waltz in the middle, slaps the princess in the face, and strides from the Bal Tabarin proclaiming — somewhat to the misgiving grunts of the American business men out front — that a man who would allow a woman to support him is one not worthy of the name; (2) nautical melodramas in which, at a sudden lull on the part of the villainous crew on the decks outside, the heroine whispers, " They're still," to which the hero, darkly wrinkling his brow, mutters hoarsely and ominously, " Yes — *too* still! "; (*3*) character clichés such as the acidulous spinster who, at the very thought of amorous passion in others, seizes up the table service and bustles bristling out of the room; the gentleman farmer surprisingly given to a fondness for playing Rachmaninoff on the piano; the physically provocative woman of foreign blood who, visiting in her husband's family's house, promptly turns his brothers' thoughts to " A Night in the Harem "; and the placid husband who dolefully allows that he is in his forties and thereby implies to the audience that he will have to stand around for the rest of the evening and watch his wife angle for sex among the younger actors in the company; (4) plays that lie themselves out of libel suits by publishing in the program a fore-note to the following effect: "The author desires to assure the audience that the characters and events in this play are entirely imaginary," when nine-tenths of the audience subsequently, and with the greatest ease, recognize most of the characters and events to have been founded upon real persons and fact; (5) musical shows in which, when the comedian hears a shot off stage, he forthwith proceeds to limp; (6) emotional actresses who indulge in a wealth of vocal and deportmental *Weltschmerz, Heimweh, Liebestraum* and *Franziskanerbräu,* all intended to convey the picture of a Duse full of pent-up artistic passion and æsthetic hops; (7) young actors who read their lines as if the last word or two in them were part of the Masonic arcanum and who begin each sentence in high feather at the top of a shoot-the-chutes and then swiftly glide down into a completely drowned utterance, all wet; (8) modern musical comedies that sentimentally hark back to the period when three-quarters of our musical exhibitions were laid in the grand salon of the château of Compte Gustave, when no chorus girl wore a satin skirt less than twelve feet in circumference, and when the big chandelier in the ball-room scene cost more than all the combined newspaper advertisements; (9) very young playwrights who are given to the characteristic juvenile habit of superiorly attributing this or that character's dubious emotional philosophy to his or her youth; (*10*) such humor as consists in a line delivered by one of the male characters to the effect that, though he has heard of the degree A.B., the only one he knows is S.O.B.; (*11*) such devices as the arousing of suspicion as to a departed visitor's identity by a remaining whiff of a familiar perfume; (*12*) the arty dance number in which Harlequin, first revealed as a puppet, slowly comes to life; (*13*) the lady in Elizabethan court costume who paradoxically sings a saucy modern ditty; (*14*) actors who, given a simple line to the effect, say, that it is raining out-of-doors, not only promptly go into an *aria di bravura* but so comport themselves physically that the spectator is not certain whether he is in a dramatic theatre or at the Olympic games; (*15*) such comedy dodges as a female character's ignorance of the meaning of some more or less familiar term and her glossing over of her discomfiture with a prompt, lofty and decisive — and absurd — definition of it; (*16*) actresses who rely upon a physiognomic pantomime, involving chiefly the *orbicularis palpebrarum* and *compressor naris* muscles, to suggest a sly malignity; (*17*) bit-actors who, on the score of a performance lasting from thirty seconds to a minute in a two-hour play, run away with the critics' acting honors by the simple expedient of remaining on the stage for so short a time that no one has a chance to find out how little of acting they really know; (*18*) humor that consists in a foreigner's difficulty in grasping the shades of English meaning as when, for example, upon a young alien's desire to tell his inamorata that he wishes to spark with her, he blurts out, " Tonight I will come and we will make sparks "; (*19*) directors who attempt to inject into musical shows the gayety they lack by causing the leading performers and the members of the chorus to issue uproarious laughs after every other spoken line and at the conclusion of each of the musical numbers; (*20*) actresses in the rôles of artistes of one sort or another who display the excessive lugubriousness associated in the old stock-company histrionic mind with the artistic temperament and affect a mien suggestive of being simultaneously with child by at least four Paderewskis, all of whom have cruelly deserted them, in their hour of pain, for Helen Morgan; (*21*) pseudo-sophisticated modern English comedies in which the heroines' rôles are occupied by trousered actors, and still others in which it is difficult to tell whether the leading woman has shown up that night or whether it is her uncle who is substituting for her; (*22*) second act scenes in which the family works itself up into a wild and terror-stricken stew over the danger to its young daughter's chastity, the latter having gone out for the evening against the family's wishes with a dubious, fashionable fellow-about-town; (*23*) the child who is injured in an accident and is carried into the scene just as the mother, all agog, is preparing at long last for one happy night out with her hard-working husband; (*24*) the young daughter who challengingly allows that she is going to lead her own life and who, just as everybody fears that the worst has happened, comes back home in drunken, but otherwise innocent, contrition; (25) the wise and breezy young woman secretary who, when the young hero seems doomed to be beaten, throws her hat into the ring, consigns her old crooked employers to the devil, and announces that she is henceforth on his side and is going to see him through; (26) the scene on the moonlit boudoir balcony with the lovers in adjoining bedrooms and the nightingale water-whistle blown allusively by a stagehand, the wife who pretends that it was she who was in her daughter-in-law's room all the while in order to confound a potential blackmailer who has caught sight of the lover on the balcony, and the doddering but gentle and understanding old scientist husband (he experiments with bugs and butterflies) who allows his wife to believe that he does not suspect her infatuation for the friend of the family, who is duly off to India in the last act; and (27) playwrights of the Nineties who seem to imagine that the way to write a modern, up-to-the-minute play is to sprinkle the dialogue with as many *bitches, bastards* and *nuts* as possible.

23

We have with us in the American theatre today a group of such elderly playwrights who, hoping against hope to keep in the swim, seem to believe that the quality of modernity consists simply either in a miscellaneous employment of the sexual epithets encountered in waterfront cat-houses and the polite comedies of Mr. Noël

Coward, or in the demotion of the human brain to a position fourteen inches due south of the umbilicus.

24

Maxwell Anderson's "Mary of Scotland" as a play disdainfully waves aside the historical facts as to its heroine and as a stage production disdainfully waves aside her recorded physical aspect. As history, accordingly, it is worthless, and as an embodied portrait of the woman herself, bogus. Yet it is here and there an interesting and, by virtue of the colors in its creator's pen, a sometimes verbally enticing theatrical exhibit. For Anderson, though he is hardly the lush poet that certain commentators would have us believe, is at least much more expert in the use and facile rhythm of words than most of his American dramatic contemporaries and, in addition, has a touch of imagination superior to the majority of them. But the difference between a Schiller and a Tennyson on the one hand and an Anderson on the other consists in the circumstance that whereas the dramas of Mary Stuart that the former have composed shoot out the gleam and glow that lie in the heart of true poetry, the drama of the latter merely flickers with its surface sheen.

It would be flimsy criticism, of course, to disallow to Anderson the privilege of converting history to his own poetical ends, provided he were able to make his ends meet. There is no more reason why he shouldn't make Mary Stuart anything from queen of Siam to the wife of Chancellor Schuschnigg — if poetic competence justified — than there is why Shakespeare shouldn't have taken a primitively minded savage, set him down into an alien century, given him a sensitive analytical mind, and constituted him the hero of one of the world's greatest dramatic tragedies. A poet's mission is to render facts spurious and sham truthful. The degree to which he is successful stamps his level as an artist. There are times when Anderson dusts off the stars, but there are others when he merely dusts off the velour robes and gilt crowns of mock-heroic drama. His play aspires to the heights, but the escalator of his blank verse that essays to carry it to the mountain top periodically lets out disturbing little creaks.

What is contended in behalf of the play itself, so far as its historical integrity is concerned, may be contended also in behalf of the casting of the diminutive Miss Helen Hayes as the relatively towering Stuart. I can see no more argument against the Theatre Guild's casting of Miss Hayes in the rôle than I can see in its casting of the Russian Madame Nazimova as the Chinese wife in "The Good Earth " or as the New England wife in " Mourning Becomes Electra." It, again, is all a question of competence or incompetence. The incompetence of Madame Nazimova made the Guild's placing of her in the rôles named — particularly the former — absurd. But while little Miss Hayes' performance is not all that might be desired of her Stuart rôle — there is a time in the second act when one anticipates, upon one's exit at the end of the evening, to

[253]

see a sign in the lobby reading, " Tomorrow night, Jackie Coogan as Hamlet " — it is in the main a task ably done, and now and then touched with some semblance of quality.

25

It has been my pretty general experience in the theatre that, when the program indicates that the evening's drama is to be laid for the major part at a long table in a committee room, assembly hall or council chamber, one may properly fear the worst. Of the numerous plays containing as their principal item of furniture a twenty-foot conference table, I have difficulty in recalling one that was all it should have been.

26

A new producing group calling itself the Theatre Union, after spending considerable money on stamps over a period of time by way of assuring me, among others, that it was going to be exceptionally hot stuff in almost all departments of the theatre, finally heaved into the arena with an exhibit by the Messrs. Sklar and Maltz named " Peace On Earth." The advisory board of the Theatre Union, I noted in the program, consisted of such eminentos as John Dos Pasoss, Lewis Mumford, Elmer Rice, Waldo Frank, Sherwood Anderson, Countee Cullen, Lynn Riggs, Roger Baldwin, Stephen Vincent Benét and Edmund Wilson. The first thing the advisory board should have advised the Theatre Union to do was not to produce " Peace On Earth."

" Peace On Earth " was a propaganda play and it is, of course, a well-known fact that all amateur or semi-amateur groups, starting off into theatrical being, invariably begin business either with a propaganda play or a bit of exotic sex delicatessen. That is, save when the group happens to be headed by some college instructor in English, in which event shop is opened up either with one of the least interesting of Björnson's plays or with Schnitzler's " Anatol " (which conveniently allows the instructor, under the guise of drama, to get in some private monkey-business with six or seven good-looking co-eds). The difficulty with " Peace On Earth," however, was not that it was a propaganda play (it would be easy to prove that nine-tenths of the world's finest dramas are, in one degree or another, propaganda plays), but that it was a propaganda play which, for all its youthful intensity and steaming sincerity, went askew and persuaded one of the exact opposite of what it intended. Aside from being a very badly written play, it was an amateurishly minded one, so amateurishly minded, in point of fact, as to be quite nonsensical. I illustrate with one example from many. The hero, a militant pacifist, along with a brother ditto, was shown reading the Declaration of Independence in a public place. A mob gathered and, aroused by the implications of the reading, proceeded to ferment, boil, and generally augur some pretty hell-raising. A policeman asked the soap-boxer to desist and thus allow the mob to disperse before trouble started. Whereupon the soap-boxer, apparently unaware of the usual municipal regulations as to permitless congresses, disturbance of the peace, inciting to riot, public nuisance, and the like, took the centre of the stage and impassionedly protested against the curtailment of free speech. " So it's a crime to read the Declaration of Independence, is it? " he indignantly proclaimed, presumably to the authors' immense delight in having put over a trenchant fast one. That, under exactly the same circumstances and conditions, it would have been an equally actionable misdemeanor to read Aesop's fables, does not seem to have occurred to the playwriting boys.

The play was full of such juvenile moonshine, including among other things a demand that the audience work itself into lather because a college bestowed an honorary degree upon its greatest benefactor, who happened to be a manufacturer of war munitions. The high significance and importance which the authors attached to honorary degrees was a sufficient indication of their intellectual and philosophical voltage. To boot, if it be argued that a decision on the part of colleges to withhold honorary degrees from men in favor of war would help to get rid of war, might it not equally be argued that a similar decision to withhold such degrees from college professors, who currently get them by the wholesale, would help to get rid of the colleges themselves?

About once in every eight years, when the theatre closes up shop, I go around and give myself a look at the New York night clubs. It having been 1926 when I took the last look, this was again my year, so I gathered about me a nocturnal stew of my acquaintance and set forth.

The night clubs, I found, have changed imperceptibly during the period of my absence. For the privilege of buying a bottle of highly charged New Jersey Sauterne promulgated as vintage Bollinger and listening to three young men in swallow-tails ten inches too long for them sing about what happened to one of their number when he wandered into the harem, you are still done out of a full year's interest on your Treasury bonds. If, thoughtlessly, you allow yourself to become slightly hungry while subsequently listening to the three young men sing about what happened to the one who had wandered into the harem when, on another occasion, he took his girl out into the woods to look, as he thought, at the wild flowers, and you order a small cheese sandwich, with or without mustard, you have to sell the bonds.

Adding to the festiveness of the evening, there is, also, still a jazz band. All the bands play exactly the same tunes. And all imagine that they induce in the customers an overpowering sexual stimulation by having the head-waiter turn down the lights and by playing so pianissimo that no one but the leaders themselves, provided they haven't bad colds in the head, can hear them. The only

ago, first negotiate a dreamy waltz, which ends with the woman drooping like a languorous lily across her partner's extended right arm, and who wind up their performance with a fox trot, which ends with the couple spinning rapidly fifteen times around the room.

Then, in the larger night clubs, there is, of course, the floor show. The only difference between the floor show of the present year and the floor show of 1926 or 1918 is the degree of undress. Where, formerly, the girls at least came out in their panties, today they come out with nothing between them and their Maker but their consciences. And any number of them, apparently, also leave off their consciences. Once on the floor, they go through much the same chorus maneuvers that galvanized the papas back in the days of " The Isle of Champagne " and " Wang," save for some very modern ensemble tap dancing of the vintage of 1912. Incidental fillips consist in having the girls throw small white cotton snow-balls at the assembled nitwits (an echo of the early Texas Guinan days), or in having them pass along the ringside tables with toy balloons, which the Lotharios seated thereat blow up with their cigarette butts (an echo of the early Ziegfeld Roof days).

Other familiar items of night club routine are the clowning master of ceremonies who delivers himself of presumably excruciating remarks at the expense of the performers and of those customers with whom he feels fairly safe in taking a chance, and the usual quota of theoretically Gallic chanteuses who wickedly roll their eyes and toss their hips the while they sing perfectly harmless ditties about luff.

28

I observe — and pass it on for what it is worth — that in the theatre of today most of the young women who are making themselves felt give out a very definite sense of personal intelligence. The day of great popularity for the young female dumb-bell and director's robot seems rapidly to be disappearing. Look over the girls who have made the biggest hits on the local stage during the last two or three years and, investigating their private records as to education, position, etc. — which isn't any of a critic's business, incidentally — you will find that they are girls with something in their heads other than the names of the best dressmakers, who's who at the Racquet Club, and the best dancer at the Mayfair shindigs. The young hollow-head who leaves school after the Third Reader and who imagines that the best way to prepare herself for dramatic eminence is to spend seven or eight years trouping dismally through Iowa and Nebraska and three or four more playing in tank-town stock companies is gradually discovering herself in the audiences' discard, however magnificent her hair dye. The increased intelligent drama of today calls for increased intelligent young women.

29

When Bourdet's " Le Sexe Faible " was first produced in Paris, it was found after the opening performance that the audience had not cottoned to it quite so wholeheartedly as had been wished. Something — something very slight — was wrong with it somewhere, but just what it was neither the author nor anyone connected with the management could put a finger on. The audience liked the play — that was plain enough — but its liking was modified by a strange, undecipherable jot of dissatisfaction. And when the second and third audiences not only showed the same peculiar dissatisfaction but also diminished in numbers, Bourdet and his colleagues were alarmed. " Maybe the sordidness of the atmosphere and of the characters' viewpoints gets a bit too depressing as the evening wears on," suggested the leading actor, Boucher. " I've got an idea. Let me try it out tonight," he urged. What his idea was, he would not confide. But that night, after he had spoken the line that had previously brought the second act to a close, he inserted another. It was — with a critical sniff at the thematic dead-cat atmosphere: " Now, let's all go out and get a breath of fresh air!" From that moment on, " Le Sexe Faible " became the outstanding hit of the Paris season.

30

One of the curses of present-day American play-writing is the desperate effort of playwrights without wit to be witty. Every now and then a comedy that might be moderately entertaining if its author allowed himself to write it simply and directly turns out to be a miserable earache because of his insistent belief that it is necessary for him to interrupt every other line of its dialogue with something, however irrelevant, that he considers ultra-snappy. It is almost impossible to go to the theatre these days and see a comedy in which — for no other reason than that the author imagines it is publicly demanded of him that he be a fellow of rich *mots* — the characters do not resolve themselves into so many vaudeville brother and sister acts, minus only the customary clog dancing.

31

That the Galsworthy drama sputtered out and died some time before its author was evident to anyone who studied his later plays. His last, " Exiled," disclosed him in a repetitious and echoful state and brought down its final curtain on the conviction that, so far as the theatre was concerned, he had completely shot his bolt. For the exhibit, dealing with Englishmen driven by the post-war turn of events from their old England, he borrowed characters outright from such of his former plays as " The Pigeon," " The Skin Game," etc., borrowed thematic devices as well, and fell back wearily at the finish upon such hokum whoopee as even our Mr. George M. Cohan long since has hesitated at. England is shown for three acts to be in a bad and even odious way. But — eleven o'clock and rococo George M. Galsworthy to the colors! "We're not in Ireland. We're in England, and thank God for it!" says the innkeeper. "Good old England; and ain't she getting old?" observes the commercial traveler. "Not *she*," returns the other; "She's a two-year-old!" "And we love 'er; and we love 'er!" adds the traveler. Whereupon Sir Charles: "Love her! That *is* the trouble. *And* the cure!" A chorus of miners' voices off-stage is heard in "John Brown's Body." "But *her* soul goes marching on!" proclaims Sir Charles.

As for humor, never Galsworthy's particular forte, the brand is several cuts below that of "Escape," which in turn was distinctly that of the vaudeville halls. I quote a few samples:

1. "I think I should be a success with lions. My canary feeds out of my mouth."

2. "I shall put my skirt on Flying Kite." "You won't lose much!"

3. "Quate! 'Ow culched! Hairs and grices! Why the 'ell can't she speak the King's English?"

4. "That picture of mine's fine; the missus says she'd know it in the dark." "Does she know it in the light?"

5. Photographer: "I shall not want his legs." Sitter: "What's the matter with my legs?" Daughter: "He's thinking of your feet of clay, dear."

6. Photographer: "If I might suggest thinking of something pleasant." Sitter: "Well, what?" Secretary: "Oysters, Sir John. Oh! dear! It's May!"

7. Sir John (*indicating bust of Julius Caesar*): " That one of George Washington's good." Sir Charles: " What a queer likeness to Julius Caesar! "

As for the clichés, we encounter such observations as " I like dogs. They're friendly things," with the rejoinder: " More friendly, I'm afraid, than human beings "; such dialogue as, " I only thought —," interrupted by, " Well, don't! " ; and such symbolism as naming the potential winning race-horse after the play's theme, Evolution.

32

Almost all the young English actors that we see on today's stage look so much alike, look so much like cut-outs from exactly the same pattern, that when two or more of them appear in the same play I become increasingly confused, as the evening wears on, in any attempt to straighten out the plot. For the same reason, I seldom can get a motion picture straight, as the actresses in most of them all look like Carole Lombard and the men all look like Ronald Colman. Who is the heroine or the adventuress or the servant-girl in a particular picture, I can't distinguish, any more than I can distinguish, as the plot unfolds, whether it is A or B or C with the little black moustache who is the hero or the villain or the iceman.

33

In the last three or four years it has been almost impossible to find a musical show of the general revue stamp that has not opened the evening either with a number in which the chorus girls chant a facetious lyric informing the audience of the standard music show items that will happily not figure in the subsequent performance or with one in which the standard characters of such a show — juvenile, comedian, sister act, hoofer, crooner, etc. — do not come out one by one and lightly ridicule their own banality. In the first instance, the hope, patently, is that the audience will subsequently imagine that it sees a novelty that is more often than not non-existent, and, in the second, that it will be so disarmed and won by the charming (if obligatorily fraudulent) frankness of the authors that it will remit its otherwise possibly harsh judgment. The authors' good luck in both cases lies in the circumstance that hardly anyone ever gets to a music show in time to hear the opening number, with the result that audiences are not prejudiced by the rank staleness of these prefatory dodges and take what the evening offers, quite simply, for better or worse.

34

Removing our critical plug hats, let us briefly meditate the motion picture phenomenon known as Mae West. In her various theatrical and dramatic manifestations there seemed to be nothing about the lady to make one rush to one's desk and grab up a pencil. Her enormous success in the mooing pictures — tidings of which had come to the play reviewers' ears — was therefore something that induced in them a wholesale and consuming curiosity. Why?, they inquired. And, inquiring, they journeyed around to have a look. That look did not do much to distil their inquisitiveness, for what they beheld was the same old Mae of " Diamond Lil," " Sex," etc., the same old Mae with the amplitudinous bosoms and hips and the even more amplitudinous — believe it or not — hinterparts. Yet the movie houses in which she was appearing were all packed to the doors with excited and admiring mobs and, at a number of them, the police had to be summoned to keep the tides of customers at the ticket windows in some faint semblance of Christian order.

What was the mystery?, the critical gentry pondered. And then, suddenly, the very probable explanation filtered into their startled consciousness. Mae West, this Mae West, *was the only woman that the talking pictures, since their advent, had disclosed to their audiences!* What the movie audiences had uniformly been privileged to see before, over a period of years, had been nothing but an endless succession of imported Lesbians, spindled-shanked, flat-chested flappers, forty-year-old Baby Dolls, beauty parlor imitations of women, and Sylvia-massaged string beans, in not one of whom there was enough real, genuine, honest-to-God female quality to interest even a vegetarian cannibal. In the midst of this dearth, the Mlle. West came like a rain-fall, a veritable torrent, upon a dry desert. Here, unmistakably, whatever anyone might think of her art, was a *woman,* a *female.* No little dried-up cutie, no pretty little narrow-shouldered skeleton of a chicken, no parched and skinny pseudo-vamp, no trumped-up, artificial siren, but a good, large, full, round, old-time, 1890-model woman, with " woman " up and down and sidewise written plainly on her every feature — and all other places.

Like some rare and strange freak, therefore, La Belle West descended upon the screen and audiences galloped to see the phenomenon. In the theatre, she attracted no especial attention, for the theatre has its full share of out-and-out women and they are no particular novelty. But the pictures were and are different. Hence the triumphant epiphany of Our Mae.

35

The chief bore of all Gilbert and Sullivan revivals is, of course, the audience. Allowing all the very great virtue to Gilbert that was unquestionably his, it still takes an epizoötic hypocrite to pretend that many of his quips and jests are not, in this day and age, woefully frayed and even discommodiously tiresome. Yet the fraudulent old Savoyards who pop out of hiding every time anything by Gilbert and Sullivan is produced still profess, with loud mechanical guffaws, to find them too overwhelmingly comical for comfort, and rend the auditorium air with their strained and suspect responses. When, for example, Don Alhambra is mistaken for an undertaker because he is dressed in black, when Gianetta dumb-shows *mal de mer,* when the Duke plays elaborately with the word *soupçon,* when Giuseppe observes, "My ideas of politeness are confined to taking off my hat to my passengers when they tip me," the Duchess replies, "That's all very well, but it is not enough," and Giuseppe comes back with, "I'll take off anything else in reason"—when, under such melancholy circumstances, only some particularly senescent Rip Van Winkle could so much as dredge up a faint smile and we yet hear a present-day audience shout their heads off in unrestrained mirth, there is obviously nothing left for us but to conclude that we are sitting in the midst of a lot of outrageously posturing fakers.

36

A word about a habit of theatre managers when the warm weather comes 'round. I refer to their leaving the exit doors of their theatres partly open during performances to let in a little theoretically cool air. What they let in may, on rare occasions, be a little cool air, but what they also let in, on all occasions, is a great deal of street noise which disturbs the audience out of all hearing of what is going on on the stage. Even if a theatrical season were not at this period of the year almost through, this custom of the house managers would go a long way toward ending it in quick order. People go to the theatre and pay out their good money to hear plays, not automobile horns, newsboys' cries, street fights, traffic racket, and other such things that they can hear at any time, gratis. When they pay out $3.30 for the pleasure of hearing Lady Frobisher

A NOTE ON THE TYPE
IN WHICH THIS BOOK IS SET

DEVELOPMENT OF

DEVICE OF
ROBERT GRANJON

This book is set in Granjon, a type named in compliment to ROBERT GRANJON, but neither a copy of a classic face nor an entirely original creation. George W. Jones drew the basic design for this type from classic sources, but deviated from his model to profit by the intervening centuries of experience and progress. This type is based primarily upon the type used by Claude Garamond (1510–61) in his beautiful French books, and more closely resembles Garamond's own than do any of the various modern types that bear his name.

Of Robert Granjon nothing is known before 1545, except that he had begun his career as type-cutter in 1523. The boldest and most original designer of his time, he was one of the first to practise the trade of type-founder apart from that of printer. Between 1549 and 1551 he printed a number of books in Paris, also continuing as type-cutter. By 1557 he was settled in Lyons and had married Antoinette Salamon, whose father, Bernard, was an artist associated with Jean de Tournes. Between 1557 and 1562 Granjon printed about twenty books in types designed by himself, following, after the fashion of the day, the cursive handwriting of the time. These types, usually known as "caractères de civilité," he himself called "lettres françaises," as especially appropriate to his own country. He was granted a monopoly of these types for ten years, but they were soon copied. Granjon appears to have lived in Antwerp for a time, but was at Lyons in 1575 and 1577, and for the next decade at Rome, working for the Vatican and Medici presses, his work consisting largely in cutting exotic types. Towards the end of his life he may have returned to live in Paris, where he died in 1590.

This book was composed, printed, and bound by The Plimpton Press, Norwood, Mass. The paper was manufactured by S. D. Warren Co., Boston.